The Lord, He is God

The Lord, He is God

Meditations on the Lives of Elijah and Elisha

Ben Stahl

The Lord, He is God
Meditations on the Lives of Elijah and Elisha
by Ben Stahl
Published by Ben Stahl, Atlanta, GA

www.LikeTheGreatMountains.com

© 2020 Benjamin Stahl

Cover art by Ben Stahl
(The Diamond on Long's Peak at Sunrise, Rocky Mountain National Park, CO)

ISBN: 9798676960384

Independently Published

To my dear wife and sons,

Although the fig tree shall not blossom,

Neither shall fruit be in the vines;

The labor of the olive shall fail,

And the fields shall yield no meat;

The flock shall be cut off from the fold,

And there shall be no herd in the stalls:

Yet may you rejoice in the Lord

And take joy in the God of your salvation!

Acknowledgments

This book came from a compilation of daily devotionals published in the spring and summer of 2020. In order to make the devotionals easier to read and grammatically correct, my dear wife spent many late nights and early mornings editing each of those devotionals for me which greatly helped in the preparation of this book. I could not have done this work without her godly wisdom, counsel, and mastery of English. I remain forever grateful that the Lord has given me a virtuous and excellent wife whose worth is well above rubies!

I must also acknowledge and thank my sons and many family members and friends who encouraged me to produce this work. May the Lord continue to use you all mightily in His Kingdom until the day of His return.

Forward

"Your mercy, O Lord, is in the heavens; Your faithfulness reaches to the clouds. Your righteousness is like the great mountains; Your judgments are a great deep..." (Psalm 36:5-6, NKJV)

My family and I have spent the majority of our vacations in the past several years at Rocky Mountain National Park in Colorado. Each year as we make plans to go back, we consult the maps and guidebooks and find new areas of the park to explore, new mountain summits to reach, and new hiking trails to conquer. The park is so large, the terrain so diverse, the views so majestic, we could probably vacation there the rest of our lives, looking forward to returning each year more so than the year before.

Paul brings Romans 11 to a close with these words from verse 33: "O, the depth of the riches both of the wisdom and knowledge of God! How unsearchable are His judgments and His ways past finding out" (NKJV). The glory of the Lord in His being, wisdom, power, holiness, justice, goodness, and truth is far beyond what our finite minds can comprehend. The infinite, eternal, and unchangeable triune God is so high above us, we cannot comprehend the fullness of His glory. But He has condescended and reached down to reveal Himself to us. The transcendent God sent His truth to us from Heaven (Ps. 57:3). He has revealed His truth to us in a book, the Scriptures of the Old and New Testaments, the Bible.

Just as we love going back to the mountains, even those we have traversed before, so we as Christians love going back to the vast mine that is the Word of God whose depth no mere man has ever reached. The mine is filled with treasure, immeasurable riches of everlasting hope and comfort, the forgiveness of sin, perfect peace, and eternal life and salvation.

In this mine of the Word of God there is a particular treasure worth more than all the rest. Some men before us have found it and some reading today will find it if they have not already. The Scripture refers to it as a pearl (Matt. 13:45-46), not just any pearl, but the pearl of greatest value. When the merchants of this world go looking for treasure in the mine and by the work of the Holy Spirit within them find this pearl, they give up everything to attain it and make it their own. This great pearl is available to all today and can still be found in the Scripture. The pearl of great price is a person. His name is Jesus Christ. He is fully God and fully man and He came to earth some 2,000 years ago to save sinners from their sins by dying on the cross to pay for their sins to the uttermost. He died for our sins. He rose from the dead on the third day. He then ascended into Heaven where He is now praying and interceding for us until He returns on the day of judgment.

The devotionals that follow were written during the Covid-19 outbreak as individual blog posts. Initially I expected to write just 10-20 before life returned to normal. As the one-hundredth approached several people suggested self-publishing as a devotional book. The devotionals begin with the call of Elijah in I Kings 17. They conclude with the raising of the Shunammite's son from the dead in II Kings 4. At times, one devotional will cover many verses of Scripture. More often though, one devotional covers just one or two verses. On more than one occasion multiple devotionals unpack just one verse. The goal is to bring readers a small taste of the depths of the riches of the Word of God through the study of the ways, works, and wonders of the Lord revealed to us in that Word. We will never explore God's Word comprehensively. Our finite mind can never comprehend the fullness of the infinite God. But in the Word we can come to know God truly and find in Jesus Christ, the Son of God, everlasting life and salvation this very day.

My hope and prayer from these simple devotionals is two-fold: First, that Christians would love the Word of God and the God of the Word more than they do today. As my family gets to know the mountains better we desire to be there more. So may we desire to be with our Lord more as we come to know His Word more. It can be easy to read over long passages of Scripture and glean great truths from them. But what of individual and perhaps overlooked verses? Jesus told the devil that man shall live by "every word that proceeds from the mouth of God" (Matt. 4:4). May the Lord give you, dear Christian, a joy in searching the depths and riches of the wisdom of God found in His Word. May we not content ourselves merely with looking at it but with eating it, being filled with it, believing it, meditating upon it, singing it, telling it to others, and being sanctified through it.

Second, I hope these devotionals will teach the truth to unbelievers so that they may repent of their sins, believe in Jesus Christ alone, and be saved. Towards that end, several devotionals speak to the follies of false religions and vain philosophies of the world. Perhaps the Lord will use these devotionals to convict and call unbelievers from lies about God to the truth of salvation by the grace of God alone received through faith alone placed in Jesus Christ alone as He is found in the Scripture alone all for the glory of God alone.

"The grass withereth, the flower fadeth: but the word of our God shall stand forever" (Isaiah 40:8).

1

Elijah

In the thirty-eighth year of Asa king of Judah, Ahab the son of Omri became king over Israel; and Ahab the son of Omri reigned over Israel in Samaria twenty-two years. Now Ahab the son of Omri did evil in the sight of the LORD, more than all who were before him. And it came to pass, as though it had been a trivial thing for him to walk in the sins of Jeroboam the son of Nebat, that he took as wife Jezebel the daughter of Ethbaal, king of the Sidonians; and he went and served Baal and worshiped him. Then he set up an altar for Baal in the temple of Baal, which he had built in Samaria. And Ahab made a wooden image. Ahab did more to provoke the LORD God of Israel to anger than all the kings of Israel who were before him. In his days Hiel of Bethel built Jericho. He laid its foundation with Abiram his firstborn, and with his youngest son Segub he set up its gates, according to the word of the LORD, which He had spoken through Joshua the son of Nun.

And Elijah the Tishbite, of the inhabitants of Gilead, said to Ahab, " As the LORD God of Israel lives, before whom I stand, there shall not be dew nor rain these years, except at my word. Then the word of the LORD came to him, saying, "Get away from here and turn eastward, and hide by the Brook Cherith, which flows into the Jordan. And it will be that you shall drink from the brook, and I have commanded the ravens to feed you there."

So he went and did according to the word of the LORD, for he went and stayed by the Brook Cherith, which flows into the Jordan. The ravens brought him bread and meat in the morning, and bread and meat in the evening; and he drank from the brook. And it happened after a while that the brook dried up, because there had been no rain in the land."

I Kings 16:29 - 17:7 NKJV

n I Kings 17 the Lord introduces us to the prophet Elijah. Elijah was a type of Christ[1] in the Old Testament in that he proclaimed the Word of God to the nation of Israel; called the people to repent of their sins and believe in the Lord; and through the power of God, carried out miracles.

Elijah came onto the historical scene during a disastrous period in Israel's history. Ahab was king and Jezebel the daughter of Ethbaal, king of the Sidonians, was his wife. The kingdom of Israel has been split in two for many years. The northern kingdom was called Israel and the southern kingdom was called Judah. The kings of Israel enjoyed one thing in common from ruler to ruler – they had all done *"evil in the sight of the Lord."* But Ahab held a special place in Israel's royal history. He had done *"more to provoke the LORD, the God of Israel, to anger than all the kings of Israel who were before him"*(16:33).

God in His mercy did not leave Israel to its own wicked devices and worship of Baal. He sent Elijah His messenger to speak God's Word. Through Elijah, the Lord told Ahab of His just judgment that would come upon Israel: There would be no rain in the land. A famine and subsequent desolation would come upon Israel because of the sins of the nation led by wicked King Ahab and his wife.

From the time of that message and throughout most of his ministry, Elijah had to hide from King Ahab. But through the famine and starvation that came upon many, the Lord provided for His servant and for His remnant in Israel. He sent ravens to bring

---

[1] Jesus Christ carries out miracles of His own power for He is fully God and fully man, in two distinct natures, and one person, forever. Neither Elijah nor any other prophet could perform miracles of their own power for they were not God but were mere men. For this reason and others Elijah and other Old Testament figures are called "types" of Christ, as they are not Christ but point people to Jesus Christ.

bread and meat to Elijah every morning and evening and encamped him by a brook that he might have water.

In the pages that follow, let us behold the wondrous works of the Lord our God through the lives of Elijah and Elisha His prophets. Our God who brings destruction and judgment upon the wicked world also shows great mercy by not destroying the world completely at this time. As in the days of Elijah, so in our day God has seen fit to give the world more time to see that He is God and to turn to Him in repentance and faith. As in the days of Elijah, so in our day God continues to care for His remnant and the sheep of His pasture.

As the Lord sent ravens with food to nourish Elijah, so the Lord nourishes us with physical food and also the spiritual food of His Word that strengthens us for the trials and afflictions of life. Let us in the days that follow *"remember the deeds of the Lord...ponder all* [His] *work , and meditate on* [His] *mighty deeds..."* (Psalm 77:11a-12) so that we, like Elijah, might be well prepared to shine brightly the light of Christ through the afflictions of this present evil age.

2

The Widow of Zarephath

*Then the word of the LORD came to him, saying, "Arise, go to
Zarephath, which belongs to Sidon, and dwell there. See, I have
commanded a widow there to provide for you." So he arose and
went to Zarephath. And when he came to the gate of the city,
indeed a widow was there gathering sticks. And he called to her
and said, "Please bring me a little water in a cup, that I may
drink." And as she was going to get it, he called to her and said,
"Please bring me a morsel of bread in your hand." So she said, "As
the LORD your God lives, I do not have bread, only a handful of
flour in a bin, and a little oil in a jar; and see, I am gathering a
couple of sticks that I may go in and prepare it for myself and my
son, that we may eat it, and die.*

I Kings 17:8-12 NKJV

Sitting 20 miles north of the ancient city of Tyre and along
the coast of the Mediterranean Sea was the famous capital
city of Sidon.[1] The tribe of Asher was supposed to have
Sidon as its northern border, which would also have been the
northwestern border of Israel had Asher conquered the land
(Joshua 19:28). Sidon was notable in the book of Kings for at least
three reasons: 1) It was a city notorious for its idol worship.[2] The

[1] Some translations spell the Hebrew word as "Zidon" instead of "Sidon."
They refer to the same place. In the present day, Sidon is a small town in
Lebanon.

[2] Idol worship was not new to Sidon in the days of Ahab nor was it a new
thing for Israelites to be attracted to their idols. All the way back in
Judges, "the children of Israel did evil again in the sight of the LORD, and
served Baalim, and Ashtaroth, and the gods of Syria, and the gods of
Zidon…" (Judges 10:6)

king not only served Baal but took the name Ethbaal which means "with Baal"; 2) Jezebel, the notoriously wicked wife of Israel's king Ahab, was the daughter of Ethbaal of Sidon; and 3) it was to Zarephath, a town of Sidon, that God sent the prophet Elijah (7:9).

Often God's manner of provision for His people changes. The brook of water that satisfied Elijah's thirst dried up. Consider all the changes in your own life in recent weeks. God did not forget Elijah and God does not forget you. Instead, God had another calling for His servant – to go to the Gentile city of Zarephath, where he would minister to and be ministered to by a widow. There in Gentile Zarephath, God had commanded a woman to care for Elijah's needs (17:9-12).

The interaction between Elijah and the widow was remarkable in light of verse 12. The woman was not merely going about her routine to care for her family but she was gathering sticks to build a fire, prepare a meal for herself and her son, "and die."

This widow was on her last meal. She was not begging bread of others, for presumably they had none to spare. She was not complaining about her situation, she was simply going to gather sticks one last time, make one last meal, and with her son wait for the cruel death by starvation. In spite of this terrible distress, when Elijah the prophet of God asked her for some water, she went to get it for him.

What amazing faith this widow had in the Lord God! No matter her circumstances she would still treat a stranger with kindness. She had faith that the Lord would provide. Even if she and her son were to die, they would die serving the Lord faithfully. The woman turns away to bring the water and Elijah gives her a further test. "Bring me a morsel of bread..."

Perhaps this reminds you of another woman of Sidon, a Syrophoenician by birth who came to Jesus in Mark 7:24-30 because her daughter was possessed by a demon. Like the widow of Zarephath, the woman in Mark confessed her low estate and pleaded with the Lord for even the crumbs of His grace to be given to her daughter. In testimony of her faith and the Lord's mercy, Jesus healed the woman's daughter.

Are you experiencing changes in God's provision today? Are you doubting God's faithfulness through this period? The Lord uses Elijah and the widow of Zarephath to teach us that the Lord our God is a faithful God. He does not leave His children or forsake them, so trust Him and be always ready to serve Him even in the difficult times you are now facing. "For the Scripture says, Whoever believes on Him will not be put to shame" (Rom. 10:11).

3

Sincerely Believe

And Elijah said to her, "Do not fear; go and do as you have said, but make me a small cake from it first, and bring it to me; and afterward make some for yourself and your son. For thus says the Lord God of Israel: 'The bin of flour shall not be used up, nor shall the jar of oil run dry, until the day the Lord sends rain on the earth. So she went away and did according to the word of Elijah; and she and he and her household ate for many days. The bin of flour was not used up, nor did the jar of oil run dry, according to the word of the Lord which He spoke by Elijah.

I Kings 17:13-16 NKJV

How sincerely do we believe the Word of God? Before us in I Kings 17:13-16 is a woman, who, having lost her husband, was preparing to make the last meal for her family before they died of starvation. To make the matter more difficult, a stranger, Elijah the prophet, came to her and told her to bring him the morsel of bread that was to be her last meal.

After the widow explained the situation, Elijah responded first with these words, "Do not fear" (vs.13).[1] Then Elijah repeated his instruction to first bring him food and revealed to her the Word of the Lord regarding her family's physical needs. The flour and oil would not be empty until the day the rain (and subsequent food) returned to the land.

---

[1]Jesus used these words often in His earthly ministry. When Jairus's servants come telling him his daughter is dead, Jesus said to him, "Do not fear, only believe." (Mark 5:35-36) When the sea threatened to destroy the ship, Jesus calmed the storm and said to the disciples, "Why are you so afraid? Have you still no faith?" (Mark 4:40)

Elijah could not take away the fear of this woman with his own words but as the prophet of God, he could give her the Word of God, which removes all fear (Psalm 56:4). The widow believed the Word of the Lord (feared the Lord), made Elijah the cake (obeyed the Lord), and her household ate for many days (received the Lord's blessing)![2]

Do we receive the Word of God like this widow who believed it? She hoped in the Word, rested in it, loved it, and obeyed it.

The Lord uses the widow of Zarephath to teach us that the Word of God is not merely 'something' that can be hoped for but that it is everything that must be hoped in.[3] The widow did not hedge her faith with doubt, denial, or skepticism, she went "all in" believing the Word of God. When you are called through great trials and great personal cost to fear the Lord you can do so with confidence and even joy in the Lord for *"He who did not spare his own Son but gave him up for us all, how will he not also with him graciously give us all things?"* (Romans 8:32)

How sincerely do we believe the Word of God?

---

[2] "He fulfills the desire of those who fear him; he also hears their cry and saves them" (Psalm 145:19). See also Psalm 115:3, Proverbs 10:27; Proverbs 14:26.

[3] Hoping in the Word of God includes hoping in the God of the Word. The Word of God and the God of the Word Jesus Christ cannot be separated. Jesus Christ is the Word made flesh (John 1:14). To deny the Word is to deny Christ. To hope in Christ is to hope in the Word. Claiming one and denying the other is to deny both. See also: Psalm 119:114, 147-148.

4

The Bread of Life

And Elijah said to her, "Do not fear; go and do as you have said, but make me a small cake from it first, and bring it to me; and afterward make some for yourself and your son. For thus says the Lord God of Israel: 'The bin of flour shall not be used up, nor shall the jar of oil run dry, until the day the Lord sends rain on the earth. So she went away and did according to the word of Elijah; and she and he and her household ate for many days. The bin of flour was not used up, nor did the jar of oil run dry, according to the word of the Lord which He spoke by Elijah.

I Kings 17:13-16 NKJV

In Matthew 16:13, Jesus asked his disciples, *"Who do people say that the Son of Man is?"* The disciples reported that some said Elijah. Why do you think some people had the wrong idea that Jesus was Elijah? Just before the Matthew 16 interaction with the disciples, Jesus had done a great miracle in chapter 15 when He fed "four thousand men, besides women and children," with only seven loaves and a few small fish. When they had eaten their fill, seven baskets of food remained. Perhaps some wrongly said Elijah because they remembered the miracle at Zarephath but forgot who actually brought about the miracle.

Elijah went to the widow of Zarephath without food in a time when the people in Zarephath were dying of starvation. He delivered to the widow the Word of God and she believed it. God then testified to His Word by miraculously preserving flour and oil all the days of the famine.[1]

Consider the type of miracle: the miraculous provision of food. We should learn from this miracle at Zarephath and Jesus's miracles of feeding thousands at a time, something of our Lord and Savior. He is the God who sustains and feeds all people. Whether from ordinary means of planting, growing, and harvesting, or extraordinary means of making more than 4,000 complete meals from a few loaves and fish, our God provides our daily bread.

However, this daily provision, as good as it is, cannot sustain us forever. We get hungry quickly after meals and at some point, food will no longer sustain our lives and we will die. The physical provision of the Lord is a great blessing, but it is limited in its benefit because it does not keep away death. Eventually, the widow and her son died, and we will die too if the Lord tarries.

So what is the Lord teaching us? The bread of this world, provided by God, does not sustain life forever. But do not be afraid, Jesus Christ is life and gives life. Only Jesus Christ is the bread of life and all who believe in Him will never hunger for life again for they will have it! *"I am the bread of life; whoever comes to me shall not hunger, and whoever believes in me shall never thirst…I am the living bread that came down from heaven. If anyone eats of this bread, he will live forever. And the bread that I will give for the life of the world is my flesh"* (John 6:36, 51).

Elijah could not feed this woman of his own power; the Lord said He would feed her, and He did. One greater than Elijah came to men some 2,000 years ago and fed 4,000 people at one time and

---

[1] This is the way the Lord works in Scripture so that we might believe. He testifies to His Word with power. Jesus does not simply tell the lame man that his sins are forgiven but rather, so that the lame man and we today would know that Jesus has power to forgive sins, He tells him to rise up and walk (Mark 2:1-12). The Lord does not merely call the widow to feed Elijah her last bread but promises to provide for her time of need, and He gives her that which He promised.

5,000 at another time. He is no mere man. He is "the Christ, the Son of the living God." (Matthew 16:16) This Jesus is life and He alone freely gives life.

May you eat of this Bread today and give thanks to God.

5

The Widow's Son (Part 1)

*Now it happened after these things that the son of the woman
who owned the house became sick. And his sickness was so serious
that there was no breath left in him. So she said to Elijah, "What
have I to do with you, O man of God? Have you come to me to
bring my sin to remembrance, and to kill my son?" And he said to
her, "Give me your son." So he took him out of her arms and
carried him to the upper room where he was staying, and laid him
on his own bed. Then he cried out to the Lord and said, "O Lord my
God, have You also brought tragedy on the widow with whom I
lodge, by killing her son?" And he stretched himself out on the
child three times, and cried out to the Lord and said, "O Lord my
God, I pray, let this child's soul come back to him." Then
the Lord heard the voice of Elijah; and the soul of the child came
back to him, and he revived. And Elijah took the child and brought
him down from the upper room into the house, and gave him to
his mother. And Elijah said, "See, your son lives!" Then the woman
said to Elijah, "Now by this I know that you are a man of
God, and that the word of the Lord in your mouth is the truth."*

I Kings 17:17-24 NKJV

Have you ever been enjoying God's mercy and kindness
when a great trial suddenly came upon you? The woman of
Zarephath understood afflictions as well as anyone. The
king of her land worshipped idols. She was a widow. She lived
during one of the greatest famines in history. She and her son had
nearly died from starvation. Then, while the Lord miraculously
provided the daily bread for her household, an illness came upon
the woman's son and he died (vs. 17).

God's mercy is very great. And yet, death still comes upon all. The Israelites ate manna in the wilderness that miraculously came to them six days of the week, and yet all of those who ate that manna died (John 6:49). The son of the woman who himself had been eating the miraculous flour and oil that never ran out suddenly died.

In her grief and sorrow, the woman cried to Elijah with questions. What do you have against me? Why did you come? Are you trying to remind me of my sin by bringing death again to my family? Grief is never so bitter as when it comes suddenly on us with the death of those closest to us.

It is possible to read this passage and think the woman is speaking sinfully, but that should not be our thought for several reasons: 1) Elijah did not rebuke the woman; 2) The Scripture does not call her grief sin; 3) She still called Elijah a "man of God;" 4) she did not react in fear nor like the Israelites did she desire a former sinful way from which the Lord had mercifully delivered;[1] and 5) she demonstrated faith in God in the middle of her grief by giving her son to Elijah (v.19).

It is more appropriate to see this God-fearing widow expressing her grief like the Psalmist in Psalm 77, *"When I remember God, I moan; when I meditate, my spirit faints...Will the Lord cast off forever, and never again be favorable? Has his steadfast love forever ceased? Are his promises at an end for all time? Has God forgotten to be gracious? Has he in anger shut up his compassion?" (vs. 3,7-9).*

---

[1] The complaining of the Israelites was sinful in that they questioned the goodness of God and therefore rebelled against Him. They cried out against His deliverance from Egypt on multiple occasions (examples: Exodus 14:11-12; 16:3), even as they saw the salvation of their God on so many occasions: Plagues in Egypt, crossing of the Red Sea; bitter water made sweet; bread from heaven; victory over their enemies. This is far different from expressing grief and asking questions in that grief as this woman did at the death of her son.

Elijah took the boy and went to the Lord in prayer. The glory of the Lord was the basis for Elijah's prayer. The prophet of God was living in this woman's home. The implication of Elijah's prayer was that if God allowed the boy to remain dead, mockery would come upon the name of the Lord. The presence of the prophet of the Lord at first seemed good but then led to death. So, Elijah made a request of the Lord: "Let this child's soul come into him again" (vs. 21).

Elijah's prayers in Kings can teach us several things: 1) Requests should be made to God according to His revealed will; 2) The goal of our requests should include the honor of the name of the Lord and the revelation of the glory of the Lord to all the world; and 3) We should come boldly to the throne of God in prayer.[2]

The Lord listened to the prayer and chose to restore this boy to life. The soul of the child came into him again and he revived.[3]

Sometimes grief and sorrow follow a time of mercy and joy. Perhaps you are facing this now. Perhaps you soon will. Perhaps coronavirus is troubling us now and something greater will trouble us shortly. Remember two things as you face these trials: 1) The widow of Zarephath was grieved and shaken but did not lose hope in her God, who did all things well; and 2) I Peter 4:12-13: *"Beloved, do not be surprised at the fiery trial when it comes upon you to test you, as though something strange were happening to you. But rejoice insofar as you share Christ's sufferings, that you may also rejoice and be glad when his glory is revealed."*

---

[2] In Matthew Henry's commentary on I Kings 17, he notes for us that this is the first time in Scripture we read of someone rising from the dead. Certainly we know that Abraham expected the Lord to do this after the sacrifice of Isaac (Hebrews 11:19) and all the Christians in the Old Testament looked forward to that hope but until I Kings 17 there is no example of the Lord raising anyone from the dead. What a tremendous comfort this would have been to the people of God.

[3] Literally in Hebrew, "to restore to life." He who had been dead has had his life restored to him.

6

The Widow's Son (Part 2)

*Now it happened after these things that the son of the woman
who owned the house became sick. And his sickness was so serious
that there was no breath left in him. So she said to Elijah, "What
have I to do with you, O man of God? Have you come to me to
bring my sin to remembrance, and to kill my son?" And he said to
her, "Give me your son." So he took him out of her arms and
carried him to the upper room where he was staying, and laid him
on his own bed. Then he cried out to the Lord and said, "O Lord my
God, have You also brought tragedy on the widow with whom I
lodge, by killing her son?" And he stretched himself out on the
child three times, and cried out to the Lord and said, "O Lord my
God, I pray, let this child's soul come back to him." Then
the Lord heard the voice of Elijah; and the soul of the child came
back to him, and he revived. And Elijah took the child and brought
him down from the upper room into the house, and gave him to
his mother. And Elijah said, "See, your son lives!" Then the woman
said to Elijah, "Now by this I know that you are a man of
God, and that the word of the Lord in your mouth is the truth."*

I Kings 17:17-24 NKJV

Two of the three Bibles I use regularly have subtitles within
each chapter of Scripture. These subtitles are often helpful
in finding a portion of Scripture, but they are not the
inspired word of God and can sometimes mislead the reader as to
the events that will follow. The title above I Kings 17:17-24 is one
of those misleading subtitles because it says, *"Elijah Raises the
Widow's Son."*

The prayer of Elijah in verse 21 concluded with these words: *"O Lord my God, let this child's life come into him again."* Elijah was a great prophet of the Lord, but Elijah was not the Lord. Elijah could pray for the soul of the boy to be returned to his body, but Elijah could not give him life. Elijah was not confused by this distinction and we do not need to be confused either.

Elijah knew the God whom he served. He knew that his God was all powerful. He knew that the God who dried up the earth, brought food from the mouths of ravens, and kept flour and oil flowing for several years was also the God who could raise the dead and one day would raise all the dead. Elijah's faith was not put to shame, for the Lord raised the widow's son.

Perhaps this account of Elijah and the widow's son reminds you of other similar accounts in Scripture. If God wills, we will get to the account of Elisha and the Shunammite woman's son who died in II Kings 4.

But there is another woman in Scripture who had an only son die. The other woman was from a small town south of Galilee called Nain. Like the woman of Zarephath the woman of Nain was also a widow. You can read the account in Luke 7:11-17. It was not Elijah or Elisha that met the widow – it was Jesus Himself.

When Jesus met this woman and had compassion on her she was not alone but much of the town was with her carrying the boy out of the city to be buried. Jesus came to the boy, touched him, and said, *"Young man, I say to you arise"* (Luke 7:14). After hearing the words of Jesus, the young man who had been dead sat up, spoke, and was alive again.

Elijah and Elisha were great prophets. But they were not Jesus Christ and were not making themselves out to be Christ. They lived to point others to Christ. Elijah prayed to God asking Him to raise the widow's son. Jesus simply spoke and told the boy to "arise." Elijah had access to the throne of grace from where the power of God came forth. Jesus, the very image of the Godhead bodily, has power in and of Himself.

One day soon, the Lord Jesus Christ will again speak with power and all the dead will rise from their graves. Those who are outside of Christ, who do not believe in His name, will rise to further judgment and torment in hell for all eternity. For this reason, all those apart from Christ are called by the Lord today to repent and believe in Jesus Christ for salvation and eternal life. Those who died in Christ will rise first and those who are living on that day will rise and together we will meet Christ in the air. Together we will worship Jesus Christ who is the Resurrection and the Life.

As you meditate on this account of the raising of the widow's son, give glory, honor, thanks, and praise to the One who raised the boy from the dead. It was not Elijah - but God Himself who gave life to that boy on that day many years ago and will give life once again to all who have died in the Lord.

7

The Widow's Son (Part 3)

Now it happened after these things that the son of the woman who owned the house became sick. And his sickness was so serious that there was no breath left in him. So she said to Elijah, "What have I to do with you, O man of God? Have you come to me to bring my sin to remembrance, and to kill my son?" And he said to her, "Give me your son." So he took him out of her arms and carried him to the upper room where he was staying, and laid him on his own bed. Then he cried out to the Lord and said, "O Lord my God, have You also brought tragedy on the widow with whom I lodge, by killing her son?" And he stretched himself out on the child three times, and cried out to the Lord and said, "O Lord my God, I pray, let this child's soul come back to him." Then the Lord heard the voice of Elijah; and the soul of the child came back to him, and he revived. And Elijah took the child and brought him down from the upper room into the house, and gave him to his mother. And Elijah said, "See, your son lives!" Then the woman said to Elijah, "Now by this I know that you are a man of God, and that the word of the Lord in your mouth is the truth."

I Kings 17:17-24 NKJV

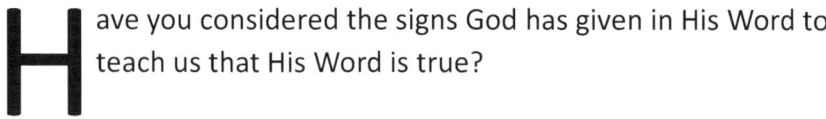 ave you considered the signs God has given in His Word to teach us that His Word is true?

Some will read the Bible and hear the gospel[1] but not believe it because they have not seen its great truth testified with miracles before their own eyes. The rich man of "The Rich Man and Lazarus" fame (Luke 16:19-31) acknowledged as much when he died in unbelief and asked Abraham to send Lazarus back from the dead to warn his brothers of the error of their ways. Abraham explained to the rich man that there was no point to sending Lazarus back from the dead because if the brothers did not believe Moses and the prophets they would not believe if someone came back from the dead. How could that statement be true?

I Kings 17 is the first account in Scripture of someone dying and rising again but it's not the only instance of this in Scripture or even in the Old Testament.[2] In Christ's parable, Abraham told the rich man that if his brothers would not believe the power of God from the Scripture of the Old Testament, they would not believe the power of God to save sinners if someone came back from the dead.

Until now, we have spent little time on the widow's final words in I Kings 24, but her words to Elijah are the conclusion of this passage and the primary lesson for us. The widow's response teaches us that because God does great works, therefore we must believe His

---

[1] The term "gospel" is used quite a lot today but may require definition. The gospel can properly be described in two parts: 1) The gospel message, simplified as:"Jesus saves" (John 1:29); and 2) The gospel call: Repent of your sins and believe in the Lord Jesus Christ and you shall be saved (Mark 1:15). This summary raises many questions, most notably, Who is Jesus Christ? What did He do? What does He save from? What is repentance? What is faith? The Bible teaches us these things as it explains to us what we are to believe about God and what duty God requires of man. The Spirit of God convinces us that all we read in the Word of God is the infallible truth.

[2] The Lord raises the Shunamite's son from the dead in II Kings 4:18-37. Later in II Kings 13, a man is buried on top of Elisha's grave and he comes back to life. The Lord promises eternal life throughout the Scripture signifying the truth of the resurrection and the Word of God.

great Word. The psalmist says in Psalm 77, *"I will remember the deeds of the Lord; yes, I will remember your wonders of old. I will ponder all your work, and meditate on your mighty deeds. Your way, O God is holy. What god is great like our God?"*

The gods of this world make many claims through their adherents, but they have never testified to their claims like the living and true God. The Lord God testifies to the truth of His Word by overpowering and defeating death itself! God testifies to His Word with power.

The widow of Zarephath saw her son who had died was raised to life again, and she believed God's Word. You and I have seen this same miracle. Will we believe the Word of God is true or will we, like the rich man, look for another authority that would exceed that of the Word?

It is unlikely that the widow of Zarephath owned even one page of Scripture in her lifetime, and yet she believed the Word of the Lord and is in Heaven today because Jesus saved her. You and I have the complete Word of God in multiple copies. At no time in history has there ever been easier or broader access to the Word of God than today. Will the widow who never even read the New Testament be in glory and someone reading this account today, be left out of Heaven because he refused to believe the Word of God? This account should provoke us to faith.

From beginning to end and especially in these passages from Kings, the reader of the Bible is inundated with the miraculous power of God, even to raise the dead. This same God, the Lord and Savior Jesus Christ, has power to forgive sins. He has forgiven all those who repent and believe in Him. If you believe the Word of the Lord today, give thanks to God that He has made Himself known to you like He made himself known to the widow of Zarephath.

8

Waiting on the Lord

*And it came to pass after many days that the word of
the Lord came to Elijah, in the third year, saying, "Go, present
yourself to Ahab, and I will send rain on the earth. So Elijah went
to present himself to Ahab; and there was a severe famine in
Samaria.*

I Kings 18:1-2 NKJV

*O God, you are my God; earnestly I seek you; my soul thirsts
for you; my flesh faints for you, as in a dry and weary land
where there is no water."*(Psalm 63:1)

I am writing this devotional in April 2020, eighteen days after I
started working from home full time. In mid-March of 2020 my
home state of Georgia put a statewide health emergency order
into effect. Yesterday, public schools were officially closed through
the balance of the school year. In Virginia, a statewide stay-at-
home order is in effect through June 10, 2020. The question on
many people's minds is how long this disease will afflict us. It does
not seem to be too great a stretch to think that such a question
was on the minds of the people of Israel as we begin I Kings 18.

Due to King Ahab leading Israel into sin, the Lord stopped the rain
in Israel (17:1). The resulting famine affected even neighboring
countries (17:12), and the famine was particularly severe in
Samaria where King Ahab resided (18:2). For three years the
famine had been on the land.

Perhaps this account reminds us of the seven-year famine in Egypt
in the days of Joseph (Genesis 41). We remember God's mercy in
that famine in giving Egypt warning of the famine and seven years

of plenty in the harvest where the Egyptians could store up provisions. There was no warning given to Baal-worshipping Israel and Sidon.

In the extended famine, the Lord did not forget His people, but in His good timing, He spoke to His prophet Elijah and told him to go to Ahab with the promise that God would send rain upon the earth. So, Elijah did as the Lord told him to do (18:2), setting up a public defeat of the followers of Baal that was recorded for all of human history.

God has not told us how long we will be afflicted with our present distress. Will 1,000 deaths per day be the height of the crisis in the United States or will it be 10,000 per day? Will He stop this affliction before the world sees its sinful ways and repents? God has not revealed these answers to us. But God has revealed to us that He hears the prayer of His people and will deliver them from their troubles (Psalm 34:17). God has revealed life and salvation through His Son and our Lord Jesus Christ.

As we continue this difficult chapter in our lives, let us look in faith and prayer to our Lord and Savior Jesus Christ who will deliver us through this present trouble.

9

He Feared the Lord Greatly: Obadiah

And Ahab had called Obadiah, who was in charge of his house. (Now Obadiah feared the Lord greatly. For so it was, while Jezebel massacred the prophets of the Lord, that Obadiah had taken one hundred prophets and hidden them, fifty to a cave, and had fed them with bread and water.) And Ahab had said to Obadiah, "Go into the land to all the springs of water and to all the brooks; perhaps we may find grass to keep the horses and mules alive, so that we will not have to kill any livestock." So they divided the land between them to explore it; Ahab went one way by himself, and Obadiah went another way by himself.

I Kings 18:3-6 NKJV

What is the responsibility of a Christian working for an employer that does wicked things? Joseph served an idol-worshipping pharaoh and was second in command in all of Egypt. Daniel served pagan rulers and was honored above all others in the kingdom. Christians in Caesar's household and centurions in Rome's army were baptized and received the Holy Spirit. Obadiah served Ahab as the ruler of his household.

Often in Scripture the Lord interrupts the "critical path" of the historical narrative to teach us a lesson of how we are to glorify God. The account of Obadiah is one of those occasions. We do not read of Obadiah any further after I Kings 18.[1] Why does the Scriptural narrative not simply bring us from Zarephath directly to the meeting between Ahab and Elijah. God intended to teach us something by placing this account of faithful Obadiah in between for all generations to read and learn from. Obadiah greatly feared God, and honored him.

The Lord used Obadiah for a very important purpose: to save 100 prophets whom Jezebel and Ahab had appointed for death. In doing so, Obadiah teaches us to fear God above men and God teaches us that He preserves His church even in the worst persecutions and pestilence.

There is no prohibition in Scripture against being employed by ungodly employers. There is a prohibition from participating in their wickedness. When the prophets of God were appointed to be killed, Obadiah at great risk to his own life not only hid 100 prophets but also fed them. The law of God supersedes the law of men. The fear of God supersedes the fear of man. *"The Lord is on my side; I will not fear. What can man do to me?"* (Psalm 118:6)

As long as Obadiah was able to follow God, he served Ahab, his master and employer. When Ahab sent him to search the land for grass for the cattle, Obadiah dutifully obeyed.

Today Christians face many temptations to serve their employers even when it means breaking God's law. Drunkenness is common at work events and dinner meetings. Christians can face mocking for drinking in moderation. Temptations to engage in licentious behavior can sometimes be faced. Temptations to take God's name in vain. Temptations to forget the holiness of the Sabbath

---

[1] Some people have claimed this Obadiah was the same man who wrote the short Old Testament book by the same name. This seems unlikely for several reasons, most notably the historical setting of the book of Obadiah and also the concern about the Edomites. Nevertheless, the Lord does not give us much information on either Obadiah, and we will have to content ourselves with learning more about these men in glory.

Day and instead to complete a work project or gain overtime abound. Temptations to support sinful causes to gain advancement in the eyes of managers. But God gives us this testimony of Obadiah to teach us that we are to fear and serve God over men. When men call us to sin against God, we must hide the law of God in our hearts and obey God like Obadiah, who hid the prophets of God and would not let them die. When we are all called to a good labor, we must do it with all our heart.

Let us seek for ourselves this legacy of Obadiah who, "feared the Lord greatly."

10

Hearing and Doing

Now as Obadiah was on his way, suddenly Elijah met him; and he recognized him, and fell on his face, and said, "Is that you, my lord Elijah?" And he answered him, "It is I. Go, tell your master, Elijah is here." So he said, "How have I sinned, that you are delivering your servant into the hand of Ahab, to kill me? As the Lord your God lives, there is no nation or kingdom where my master has not sent someone to hunt for you; and when they said, 'He is not here,' he took an oath from the kingdom or nation that they could not find you. And now you say, Go, tell your master, Elijah is here! And it shall come to pass, as soon as I am gone from you, that the Spirit of the Lord will carry you to a place I do not know; so when I go and tell Ahab, and he cannot find you, he will kill me. But I your servant have feared the Lord from my youth. Was it not reported to my lord what I did when Jezebel killed the prophets of the Lord, how I hid one hundred men of the Lord's prophets, fifty to a cave, and fed them with bread and water? And now you say, "Go, tell your master, Elijah is here." He will kill me!" Then Elijah said, "As the Lord of hosts lives, before whom I stand, I will surely present myself to him today." So Obadiah went to meet Ahab, and told him; and Ahab went to meet Elijah.

I Kings 18:7-16 NKJV

H ave you ever served the Lord faithfully in difficult times hoping for the Lord to grant relief when instead He gave you an even more dangerous or difficult task?

From man's perspective, Obadiah was playing a dangerous game. He had been disobeying the wicked orders of the king and queen, securing enough food each day to feed 100 prophets, all while managing the household of the king of Israel. After three years of severe famine, Obadiah was on a job with King Ahab to find favorable fields for some of the last surviving cattle to graze on. It was in this setting that Elijah met Obadiah and gave him a task that could have brought Obadiah to a swift death, resulting in the deaths of God's prophets as well.

Clearly when Obadiah saw Elijah it had been some time since their last meeting. Perhaps it was three years earlier when Elijah first spoke to Ahab of the drought and famine. The way Obadiah greeted Elijah is very respectful, "Is it you, my Lord Elijah?" (vs. 7). He did not ask Elijah what took him so long to come or what he had been doing; he recognized Elijah as the prophet of the Lord and honored him.

After this greeting, Elijah gave Obadiah a disheartening task. He told Obadiah to tell Ahab that Elijah was there to speak with him. The text reads almost like Obadiah broke down at this news. So hard had been his work in protecting the prophets and his own life that this new unpleasant task seemed too much to bear.

Obadiah knew that God was sheltering Elijah from the hand of the king. Elijah was at the top of Ahab and Jezebel's most wanted list. If Obadiah delivered the news to Ahab, Elijah could simply disappear again and Ahab's wrath would be taken out on Obadiah.

Have you ever been overwhelmed by the tasks the Lord has set before you? Obadiah certainly was at this moment, for he reminded Elijah of his service to the Lord from his youth to the present day (v. 12). He reminded Elijah of his protection of the 100 prophets of the Lord. The conclusion then was this question: did Elijah wish for Obadiah to be killed (v. 14)?

From verses 9-14, Obadiah laid out his concern for his pending death if he were to follow through with Elijah's command. Elijah consoled his friend Obadiah very simply with one sentence: "As the Lord of hosts lives, before whom I stand, I will surely show myself to him [Ahab] today" (vs. 15). With that, Obadiah left the narrative of Scripture and he did so in a glorious manner – he obeyed the voice of the Lord through Elijah and went and told King Ahab.

God can call you to difficult tasks followed by even more fearful tasks. He certainly did this to His servant Obadiah. But it was through this great task that the Lord would work deliverance in Israel from the plague of famine and from the plague of Baal and his priests. The most fearful time in Obadiah's labors for the Lord came right before the greatest deliverance.

Perhaps we have felt that we have labored much for the Lord during our days, and now the Lord has separated us from worshipping God together in His church. We can only see each other through electronic means. What more could the Lord have for us to do? Does He want us even now to die? Maybe. But perhaps the Lord is using this time to bring great reformation and revival in His bride, the church. Perhaps He is using it to reveal to us our secret and hidden sins and to turn us from them in repentance and faith in Jesus Christ.

Through every call of duty to the Lord may we be like Obadiah, hearing the Word of the Lord and doing it.

11

The Troubler of Israel

Then it happened, when Ahab saw Elijah, that Ahab said to him, "Is that you, O troubler of Israel?" And he answered, "I have not troubled Israel, but you and your father's house have, in that you have forsaken the commandments of the Lord and have followed the Baals. Now therefore, send and gather all Israel to me on Mount Carmel, the four hundred and fifty prophets of Baal, and the four hundred prophets of Asherah, who eat at Jezebel's table."

I Kings 18:17-19 NKJV

Seventy-one percent of Rome (10 of 14 districts) burned to the ground in the year 64 AD. The historian Tacitus said that Nero sat outside the city playing a fiddle while Rome burned. After the fire was extinguished, Nero blamed the fire on those he hated the most, Christians.[1]

When Ahab saw Elijah for the first time after three years of famine, Ahab's greeting is shocking to read: "Is it you, you troubler of Israel?" (v. 17). The king who did more evil than anyone before him (16:30), who married Jezebel, who hunted the Lord's prophets and killed them, who built altars to Baal, this Ahab had the audacity to call Elijah the "troubler of Israel." Do you see the total

---

[1] Even today it is not uncommon for the world to be hostile towards Christians during the troubles that we face. www.nationalreview.com/corner/coronavirus-relief-bill-de-blasio-media-criticize-samaritans-purse/

depravity[2] of man apart from Christ? Apart from Christ, we are unable to do good, unable to think righteously, full of deceit and guile, and able to shake our fist in anger at the holy, righteous, and almighty God.

Elijah, the prophet of the Lord, corrected Ahab's backwards mind by telling him, *"I have not troubled Israel, but you have...because you have abandoned the commandments of the Lord and followed the Baals"* (vs. 18). All who abandon the commandments of God will trouble their own homes and nations.

The text does not give any suggestion that Ahab responded to Elijah's rebuke. Instead Elijah tells Ahab to gather all Israel at Mt. Carmel along with 450 prophets of Baal and 400 prophets of Asherah for a great event in the history of Israel.

Ahab's false accusation of Elijah should remind us of another false accusation in Luke 23:1-5 when the elders, the chief priests, and scribes together brought Jesus before Pilate and accused him in this way: *"We found this fellow perverting the nation and forbidding to give tribute to Caesar, saying that he himself is Christ, a king"* (Luke 23:2). The word in Greek for "perverting"(some translations say "misleading") means to "distort," "to oppose," "plot against," "corrupt." This was the word they used to accuse Jesus.

This false accusation of the righteous God-Man Jesus Christ was terrible beyond all else. Yet, as in the days of Ahab and Elijah, the Lord would use the false accusations against Jesus for the glory of

---

[2] Total Depravity refers to the state of mankind apart from Christ, flowing from such verses as Romans 3:10-18 (itself quoting several Psalms): *"There is none righteous, no, not one: There is **none** that understandeth, there is **none** that seeketh after God. They are all gone out of the way, they are together become unprofitable; there is **none** that doeth good, no, **not one**..."* The great miracle of redemption and salvation by Christ is on display against the total depravity of men. Jesus Christ took dead men and women and made them alive in Christ Jesus. (Bold added for emphasis)

His name and the salvation of all His people. Let it be known to us and to all that *"Jesus Christ of Nazareth, whom you crucified, whom God raised from the dead...This Jesus is the stone that was rejected by you, the builders, which has become the cornerstone. And there is salvation in no one else, for there is no other name under heaven given among men by which we must be saved." (Acts 4:10-12).*

12

Two Opinions

*So Ahab sent for all the children of Israel, and gathered the
prophets together on Mount Carmel. And Elijah came to all the
people, and said, "How long will you falter between two opinions?
If the Lord is God, follow Him; but if Baal, follow him." But the
people answered him not a word.*

I Kings 18:20-21 NKJV

When the Boston Red Sox play the New York Yankees, TV
ratings, ticket prices, and media attention skyrocket.
The rivalry between the two teams goes back more
than four generations. A great rivalry existed in Israel during the
days of Elijah. It was a rivalry between the worshippers of Baal and
the prophets of the Lord. As with a major sports rivalry in our day,
the whole nation of Israel came out to see the showdown on
Mount Carmel. Unlike with sports rivalries, the souls and lives of
many people were at stake on that great day.

For too long in Israel the idolatry had been egregious. The people
practiced a form of syncretistic idolatry, combining paganism and
outward worship of the true God into one new system. Any time
we claim to love Christianity and Jesus Christ while also adhering
to false gods or philosophies of men, we are practicing
syncretism.[1] In Israel the people gave some sort of lip service to

---

[1] The Masons have the "Great Architect of the Universe," who may be
reached through all religions. Modernism seeks to find the best in each
religion and promote it accordingly. Secularists may claim Jesus while
pursuing wealth and pleasure as much or more than Christ. Syncretism
and idolatry are all around us and even within our own hearts. May we
bow the knee to Christ Jesus alone and renounce all other allegiances.

the Lord while also bowing down to Baal. Only seven thousand in all of Israel had not engaged in Baal worship (19:18).

Elijah rebuked the Israelites for their irrational practices. Either Baal was god or the Lord was God but they could not both be gods. In giving allegiance to both they had allegiance to neither. They were stuck between two opinions: 1) the opinion of the prophets of Baal; and 2) the opinion of the prophets of the Lord. The Lord God of the Bible is a jealous God. Like a husband will not accept his bride playing wife to another man, neither will the Lord God accept His bride the church giving worship to a false god. The Israelites were treating gods like investments. They didn't know which was better, so they held both to diversify and hedge and escape persecution. So Elijah challenged them to stop their foolishness and choose one god. If Baal is god, follow only him. But if the Lord is God, then follow Him.

Those who love the Lord God must be faithful to worship Him alone in the way He delights to be worshipped. This is the heart of the first and second commandment and the first and second petition of the Lord's Prayer. The Lord is jealous for His name, and His people must be jealous for His name.[2] If someone is stuck between two opinions, between two religions, between two gods, he may have many things but he does not have the true and living God as his God. The Christ of Scripture and the Christ of our own imagination, or the Christ of Scripture and Vishnu, or the Christ of

---

[2] Elijah was very jealous for the name of the Lord (19:10, 14). How much more is the Lord God jealous when His bride the church exchanges the truth of God revealed in His Word for images and foolish creations of created men? There are many vain imaginations of our God Jesus Christ in churches around the world. Images are set up as things to "assist" in worship and "art" is displayed with the intention of reminding us of God or to give honor to God. What could honor God less than false art and fake images of the true and living God? He who is the express image of the Godhead bodily cannot be represented with images of our own making. May the Lord lead His church away from lies and the provocation of the mighty God and back to the Lord. (More to come on this later.)

Scripture and anything else, will leave us stuck between two opinions and dead in our trespasses to sin. We must come to Christ as the Lord alone.

In the coming verses God will show His power and glory over the foolish idols of the world and their priests. As we consider these verses and the great event that took place at Mt. Carmel let us behold the glory and supremacy of the Lord God alone and meditate on this verse from Isaiah 46:9, *"Remember the former things of old; for I am God and there is none else; I am God and there is none like me."*

13

The Challenge

Then Elijah said to the people, "I alone am left a prophet of the Lord; but Baal's prophets are four hundred and fifty men. Therefore let them give us two bulls; and let them choose one bull for themselves, cut it in pieces, and lay it on the wood, but put no fire under it; and I will prepare the other bull, and lay it on the wood, but put no fire under it. Then you call on the name of your gods, and I will call on the name of the Lord; and the God who answers by fire, He is God." So all the people answered and said, "It is well spoken." Now Elijah said to the prophets of Baal, "Choose one bull for yourselves and prepare it first, for you are many; and call on the name of your god, but put no fire under it."

I Kings 18:22-25 NKJV

*T*hrough God we shall do valiantly: for he it is that shall tread down our enemies. *Psalm 60:12*

The enemies of God were plentiful that day on Mount Carmel when Elijah appeared as the only prophet of God in opposition to Ahab and 450 prophets of Baal.[1] The audience was tremendous as Scripture says, "Ahab sent to all the people of Israel" (18:20). We should notice the control that the Lord granted Elijah in this situation. Elijah, by the mouth of God, called for the meeting, set the location of the meeting, and determined who would attend the meeting. And they all came.

---

[1]450 prophets of Baal were present, but the original command was also for 400 prophets of Asherah. These additional 400 are not mentioned later in the chapter, so their involvement in this episode is not known.

After he rebuked the irrational and irreconcilable practices of Israel (worshipping two gods), Elijah presented a public challenge. There would be two bulls given, one for the prophets of Baal and one for Elijah, the sole prophet of the Lord. There would be wood for two altars. But, most importantly, there would not be any fire to burn the sacrifice. The prophets of Baal would call on their god and Elijah would call on the name of the Lord. Whichever God answered the prayer of His prophet(s) with fire, that would be the only true God.

Israel saw the wisdom of this challenge and publicly acknowledged that the challenge was well established. It was fair and effective, able to determine for all of Israel who was the true God.

Furthermore, the challenge was set in favor of the priests of Baal. The priests of Baal would have their pick of the two bulls and would go first. With 450 priests and the right to go first without even a coin toss, the challenge was heavily, from man's perspective, skewed in their favor. If Baal answered with fire the challenge would be completed before Elijah even had a chance to pray.

We should never be disheartened when the wicked seem to have the advantage. As Christ was taken by the chief priest's guards in the garden, led to Pilate, condemned to the cross, nailed to the tree, pierced in the side, and buried in the tomb, it seemed that death had gained its greatest victory. However, anyone who thought this had forgotten the words of Jesus when He said of His life, *"no man taketh it from me, but I lay it down of myself. I have power to lay it down, and I have power to take it again"* (John 10:18). Three days later, Jesus Christ rose from the dead defeating death and sin for all His people. In the greatest hour of evil, the greatest victory of righteousness was won.

The Lord is triumphing over the wicked today and will triumph over the wicked again. Though they may seem strong at the moment, in the great day of the Lord every knee will bow and every tongue will confess, and the glory, honor, and power of the Lord Jesus Christ will be revealed not just to one nation gathered on a mountaintop but to the whole world.

14

Is He Relieving Himself?

*So they took the bull which was given them, and they
prepared it, and called on the name of Baal from morning even till
noon, saying, "O Baal, hear us!" But there was no voice; no one
answered. Then they leaped about the altar which they had made.
And so it was, at noon, that Elijah mocked them and said,
"Cry aloud, for he is a god; either he is meditating, or he is busy, or
he is on a journey, or perhaps he is sleeping and must be
awakened." So they cried aloud, and cut themselves, as was their
custom, with knives and lances, until the blood gushed out on
them. And when midday was past, they prophesied until
the time of the offering of the evening sacrifice. But there was no
voice; no one answered, no one paid attention.*

I Kings 18:26-29 NKJV

"Perhaps Baal hasn't sent fire because he has been on
the toilet?" The Lord had a sense of humor when He
sent Elijah by himself to battle against 450 prophets of
Baal. Elijah used language on Mount Carmel used nowhere else in
Scripture to mock the foolish prophets of a foolish idol.

The folly of the priests of Baal is staggering. In hundreds of years
of receiving worship, Baal had never performed one deed great or
small. Baal was an idol made of stone. It had a mouth but could
not speak; eyes but could not see; ears but could not hear; a nose
but could not smell; hands but could not feel; feet but could not
walk; it could not make a sound in its throat, and those that
trusted in this idol became like the idol itself (Psalm 115:4-8).

Despite Baal's perfect history of doing nothing except bringing pain and misery to its followers, when the 450 prophets of Baal were presented with the impossible challenge, they accepted it. They cried all day from morning until noon, screaming "O Baal, answer us!" (19:26). But no answer came, no voice was heard. Such is the folly of those who go seeking after other gods. They are left helpless and hopeless in their hour of need. No one hears them.

Rather than give up at the end of the morning, the prophets continued into the afternoon with new fervor, even cutting themselves with swords and knives until blood gushed out upon them "after their custom" (vs. 28).[1] This is the requirement of the gods of the world, torture of the flesh in hope of receiving a favorable response that will never come.

All day they "raved on" (18:29), even until the time of the evening sacrifice to the Lord, but there was no voice, no one answered, no one paid attention, and most certainly, there was no fire. As the day ended, the prophets of Baal may have been passing out from loss of blood and running around. Their reward for such deeds was to be a picture for all of history of the folly of idol worship.

During the day, Elijah was not silent. He waited until noon watching the spectacle, but then he began to loudly mock the prophets of Baal. He taunted them and their god. Elijah suggested that perhaps Baal was talking to someone, or on the toilet, or on a journey, or asleep (18:27).

God reserves greater condemnation for those who lead others astray, and Elijah demonstrated that at Mount Carmel. Elijah rebuked the foolish Israelites for their foolish ways, but he mocked

---

[1] This reminds us of the child sacrifices made to the god Molech (Jeremiah 32:35); the torture plans of Nebuchadnezzar for those who did not bow down in the plains of Dura (Daniel 3); and the madness of the people at Ephesus who worshipped Diana and screamed for hours (Acts 19:28-34).

and scorned the wicked prophets of Baal. Jesus interacted with Israel in much the same way during His ministry. He saved His most critical judgment for the leaders of Israel; the Pharisees, Scribes, and Sadducees. But to the wretched sinner, He most often taught them and gently called them to repentance and faith.

Elijah's taunts reflect a theological point about the true God that we must not miss as we draw closer to the climax of the battle at Mount Carmel. The true and the living God never slumbers or sleeps. He always hears the cry of His children and answers them. The gods of the world, whether they be stone idols or an image supposedly of Jesus Christ Himself, will never answer. They cannot answer. They are simply idols, the creation of men's hands. *"Yea, one shall cry unto it, yet can he not answer, nor save him out of his trouble"* (Isaiah 46:7b). Let us repent of such foolishness in our own lives and look in faith to the Lord Jesus Christ, who is not silent but has spoken in His Word by His Spirit and who answers the prayers of His people.

15

Preparations for the Sacrifice

Then Elijah said to all the people, "Come near to me." So all the people came near to him. And he repaired the altar of the Lord that was broken down. And Elijah took twelve stones, according to the number of the tribes of the sons of Jacob, to whom the word of the Lord had come, saying, "Israel shall be your name." Then with the stones he built an altar in the name of the Lord; and he made a trench around the altar large enough to hold two seahs of seed. And he put the wood in order, cut the bull in pieces, and laid it on the wood, and said, "Fill four waterpots with water, and pour it on the burnt sacrifice and on the wood." Then he said, "Do it a second time," and they did it a second time; and he said, "Do it a third time," and they did it a third time. So the water ran all around the altar; and he also filled the trench with water.

I Kings 18:30-35 NKJV

Since the resurrection of Jesus Christ, many have posited theories to deny the reality of that resurrection. Some have suggested that Jesus merely passed out on the cross but did not die (the "swoon theory"). Others have suggested that the disciples stole Christ's body from the tomb at night and then claimed resurrection. These theories reach the heights of folly when compared with the accounts given in Scripture related to Christ's death and burial. He was pierced in the side after his death, and blood and water came out (John 19:34). Roman soldier guarded His tomb (Matthew 27:62-66). These things took place so that we might not be led astray with idle tales but might believe on the Lord Jesus Christ who rose from the dead in the flesh.

As the resurrection of Christ was above reproach, so was the fire from heaven at Mount Carmel. Elijah gave every advantage to the priests of Baal. They went first, they chose the bull, they had all day for Baal to answer and nothing happened. No one answered.

Then it was Elijah's turn. He had at least two objectives in his own preparations: 1) to remind the people of the glory, power, and might of the Lord God alone; and 2) to leave all in attendance and us today without any question about what took place on Mount Carmel.

Elijah began by rebuilding the altar of the Lord that had been broken down sometime in the past. He took twelve stones according to the number of Israel's tribes built an altar with them. This reminds us of the faithfulness of God. Though Israel had long since abandoned God, He had not forgotten His covenant promises to Abraham, Isaac, and Jacob.

Next Elijah built a trench around the altar, laid the wood and the slaughtered bull on it, and commanded for water to be poured on top.[1] Elijah had four barrels filled with water and poured three separate times. The twelve barrels of water did not just soak the sacrifice but *"ran around the altar and filled the trench also"* (18:35).

Elijah was showing Israel that there was no trickery on that altar. There was no fire already prepared. The sacrifice, the altar, and the trench around it were filled with water. As he completed the

---

[1] The word for the water containers is translated as "four jars" (ESV) and "four barrels" (KJV). Matthew Henry suggests the water came from the Mediterranean Sea, which, according to the Encyclopedia Britannica, touched the slopes of Mt. Carmel. The same Hebrew word translated barrels or jars is used to describe the jar Rebecca carried when she met the servant of Abraham and drew water for him and his camels (Gen. 24). The word seems to be used for a variety of jar sizes, perhaps as much as 5 - 20 gallons in each jar. Multiply that by 4 jars and each time water was poured on the sacrifice it was 20-80 gallons per time. At three times, the amount of water was likely between 60 and 240 gallons.

preparation for the sacrifice and he prepared to pray, Elijah had seriously handicapped himself.

The Lord is teaching us that His power exceeds all that can be found in the world He created. He made the world to work according to His divine decree, but He has power to work above the order He created. He can make a bush to burn but not be consumed. He can make a pillar of fire to stand in the sky without a fuel source. He can die on the cursed cross, be buried for three days, and rise again from the dead. He can ascend into Heaven and descend to Earth at the last day of His own power. What chance does a sacrifice sitting in a small pond have against the fire coming from Him who can and did do all these things? The Lord God of Elijah, our God, has all power in Heaven and in Earth, and every substance and will of man that might seek to thwart Him will only make His work more glorious when it comes to pass.

16

The Prayer of Elijah

*And it came to pass at the time of the offering of the evening
sacrifice, that Elijah the prophet came near and said, "Lord God of
Abraham, Isaac, and Israel, let it be known this day that You
are God in Israel and I am Your servant, and that I have done all
these things at Your word. Hear me, O Lord, hear me, that this
people may know that You are the Lord God, and that You have
turned their hearts back to You again."*

I Kings 18:36-37 NKJV

T he eyes of all Israel were fixed on Elijah the prophet. He
had mocked the prophets of Baal, rebuilt the altar of the
Lord, and thoroughly soaked his sacrifice with water. How
would Elijah pray to the Lord?

Elijah's short prayer in verses 36 and 37 teaches us about his
actions on Mount Carmel, his desires as a prophet in Israel, and
the goal that our prayers should have.

First, Elijah's great concern as the prophet of God was that the
people did not know God as He truly was and is. They offered lip
service to him, they acknowledged His name, but they killed His
prophets and worshiped idols. They did not "know" God, for if
they had known Him they no doubt would have worshiped Him

alone.[1] So Elijah prayed about his concern: *"Let it be known this day that thou art God in Israel... Hear me, O Lord, hear me, that this people may know that thou art the Lord God..."*

Second, the goal of the prayer matched the desire of the prophet, that God's name would be known and revered. This prayer should remind us of the preface and first petition of the Lord's Prayer. Elijah went to the Lord as the covenant God, the Father of Abraham, Isaac, and Jacob ("Our Father which art in Heaven"), and he called on the Lord to make His name known to Israel that they might worship the Lord God ("Hallowed be Thy name").

Third, his prayer revealed to Israel that Elijah was not working on his own but that the Lord had called him to be His servant. Even the mocking of the prophets of Baal and certainly the drenching of the sacrifice with water were of the Lord. Because all this was of the Lord and Elijah had done all these things at God's Word, it meant God had done these things for His people Israel. God had sent Israel a messenger, a prophet, to show again His mercy and His truth to His people who had again wondered from His ways. If the people did not know Elijah was God's servant, they could not begin to know the Lord God he preached was the only living and true God. The Israelites had left their first love, but God had not left His.

---

[1] It seems to me we face similar times in our churches. Many are giving lip service to the Lord while giving some measure of devotion to images made with human hands. Many churches have erected paintings, carvings, and other forms of images of what they claim to be the second person of the Trinity, Jesus Christ Himself. Do we not know the Lord God as He truly is anymore? He who despises worship through or with images, He who is jealous for His own name and glory alone, will He hear the prayer of those bringing idols into the sanctuary of the Lord or into the sanctuary of their own hearts? May God be pleased to use the remembrance of Elijah the prophet to cause His people to cast away every device and imagination of man that would take us from knowing the true God.

Jesus prayed similarly in John 17, "*Father, the hour has come; glorify your Son, that the Son also may glorify you: since you have given him authority over all flesh, to give eternal life to all whom you have given him. And this is eternal life, that they know you, the only true God, and Jesus Christ whom you have sent* (17:1-3).

If one does not know Jesus Christ as He truly is then one cannot know the Father. No one has the Father without the Son or the Son without the Father, for the Father and the Son are one. No one can come to the Father except through the Son. We must know Christ to have eternal life.[2]

As we think about Elijah's prayer on that great day on Mount Carmel, may the Lord grant the desire of our heart in prayer to be the glory and knowledge of the Lord that we might see the words of the prophet Habakkuk 2:14 come to pass: "*For the earth shall be filled with the knowledge of the glory of the Lord as the waters cover the sea.*"

---

[2]See I John 2:22-23; John 10:30; John 14:6; and John 17:3.

17

The Lord Vindicates His Name

Then the fire of the Lord fell and consumed the burnt sacrifice, and the wood and the stones and the dust, and it licked up the water that was in the trench.

I Kings 18:38 NKJV

From the garden of Eden to the porches of Pharaoh's palace, to the cross on Calvary itself and to the present day, the gods of the world and their followers have been at war with God Himself. Yes, they will persecute His prophets, enslave His people, profane His sacraments, and mock His Word but they do these things for the primary reason that they hate God. But God will not be mocked and His name will not be polluted. He made Dagon to fall over on his face before the ark of the covenant (I Samuel 5); the Assyrian army to lose 186,000 overnight (II Kings 19); Herod to be eaten by worms (Acts 12:18-25); and fire to come down from heaven on Mount Carmel.

The great test had come. Who is the true and the living God, Baal or the Lord? Baal had been proved utterly worthless and less than nothing by his own priests. Elijah had prepared an elaborate sacrifice, but the Lord had not yet done anything. Would the Lord demonstrate His glory on Mount Carmel? Elijah prayed for the people to know that the Lord was God and that He still heard the cry of His people in Israel.

The fire of the Lord immediately fell (vs. 38)! It did not start on the altar, it fell from the heavens. The fire did not merely consume the sacrifice of the bull, it consumed the wood, the stones, and the dust. All the water that was in the trench and over the sacrifice was licked up. This altar that was broken down would not be used again, for it was consumed on this day.

The contrast between the Lord and Baal is obvious but warrants emphasis. The prophets of Baal ran, leapt, shed their blood all day crying out to Baal and he never answered. The Lord God of Israel immediately answered with prayer. He was not "out for a walk" or "using the toilet" or "sleeping." He who neither slumbers nor sleeps answered the cry of His servant in dramatic fashion.

As the fire came down from heaven, the fear in Ahab and the prophets of Baal in particular must have been great. With such a consuming fire, Elijah who was close to the altar (vs. 36) was not harmed in the least. The Lord's name was publicly vindicated again in front of a great jury - the whole nation of Israel.

The Lord's name will again be vindicated with great fire like the fire on Mount Carmel. It will not be a fire that consumes only an animal sacrifice and its altar but a fire that will consume the whole world. *"But the day of the LORD will come like a thief, and then the heavens will pass away with a roar, and the heavenly bodies will be burned up and dissolved, and the earth and the works that are done on it will be exposed. Since all these things are thus to be dissolved, what sort of people ought you be in lives of holiness and godliness, waiting for and hastening the coming of the day of God, because of which the heavens will be set on fire and dissolved, and the heavenly bodies will melt as they burn!" (2 Peter 3:12)*

Will we be like the prophets of Baal and continue holding to our vain hopes or will we confess our sin before the Lord in faith looking with eagerness to the great day of the Lord when Jesus Himself will descend?

18

"The Lord, He Is God"

"Now when all the people saw it, they fell on their faces and said, "The LORD, He is God; the LORD, He is God."

I kings 18:39 NKJV

What is your response to reading of God's creating all things of nothing in the space of six days and all very good? What is your response to two million Israelites pressed against the Red Sea with the Egyptian army at their heels when the Lord parted the Red Sea, led His people across on dry land, and destroyed Pharaoh's army? What is your response to the falling walls of Jericho; Gideon and his 300 defeating the Midianites; Samson cutting down 1,000 Philistines with a jawbone; David killing Goliath with a sling and stone; and the widow's son being raised from the dead?

When God sent the fire from heaven for all Israel[1] to see, most people responded by falling down on their faces before Jehovah

---

[1] The great fire from heaven was unlike anything seen in that generation. God chose to reveal His glory and might on a mountain in the northern part of Israel bordering the Mediterranean Sea. It is likely that in addition to Israel, the residents of Tyre and Sidon could have seen the fire. Perhaps even the widow and her son in Zarephath could see the fire, along with sailors from many different nations who would have been on the Mediterranean Sea. As one reader noted, even Jezebel may have seen the fire from her home in Jezreel. Great was the revelation of the Lord on that day.

God and confessing with their mouths, *"The Lord, He is God; the Lord, He is God."*[2]

This was the message Elijah had preached for many years. It was the message that Elisha would preach after Elijah. This is the message of every faithful minister of the gospel and the confession of every child of the Lord: "The Lord, He is God." This declaration should remind us of Peter's good confession of Jesus, *"You are the Christ, the Son of the living God"*; the centurion's confession at the death of Jesus, *"Truly this man was the Son of God"*; that which every tongue will confess, *"Jesus Christ is Lord"*; and the words of the herald angel, *"There has been born for you a Savior, who is Christ the Lord."*

Instead of consuming the sinful people with fire on Mount Carmel, God, who is rich in mercy and abundant in grace, consumed the sacrifice with fire and brought many people to salvation. You and I should have suffered and died for our sins, but God sent His own Son to die in our place so that we might be saved.

Some have pointed out that Israel did not at this point confess the Lord as "their" God. Nor did they confess that the Lord is the "only" God. However, given Elijah's challenge of vs. 23, the clear implication was that the God who sent fire was God alone. Keil and Delitzsch note in their commentary that the meaning of the Hebrew is "Jehovah is the true or real God," in comparison to Baal and all other gods. They are fake, they are false, Jehovah God is God alone. Certainly on that day there were those confessing falsely and those (Ahab and the prophets of Baal) who did not confess at all. To them the demonstration of God's power was a ministry of judgment. But to the many others who that day were converted, the power of God was ministered to their salvation.

---

[2] When Moses and Aaron offered the sin, burnt, and peace offerings in Leviticus 9:22-24, they went into the tabernacle and the Lord sent fire from heaven and consumed the sacrifice. The people saw it, shouted, and responded by falling on their faces in worship.

In the prior chapter we saw the miracle of the fire falling from heaven. Today we see the miracle of dead men given new life. Many Israelites believed on Mount Carmel because they saw the power of God with their eyes. You and I see the power of God by faith as we read the Word of God and He testifies of it to us by His Spirit. Blessed are you who have not seen with your eyes and yet have believed. From this day and forever may we confess that the Lord, He is God; the Lord, He is God!

19

God's Judgment on His Enemies

And Elijah said to them, "Seize the prophets of Baal! Do not let one of them escape!" So they seized them; and Elijah brought them down to the Brook Kishon and executed them there.

I Kings 18:40 NKJV

I n the late 19th and early 20th centuries a new religion appeared within the walls of Protestant churches that rejected the inerrancy of Scripture, Christ's miracles, the bodily resurrection of Jesus Christ, the substitutionary atonement of Christ on the cross, and the virgin birth.[1] In the place of the teachings of Scripture were teachings on the brotherhood and goodness of man, including some good but not exclusively biblical principles. Other religions and other gods were no longer viewed as leading souls to hell but expressions of other faiths, which Christianity could praise and learn from. Missionaries no longer sought to make disciples of Jesus Christ in every nation but sought to help pretty good men and women become even better.

Today it is not uncommon for Christians to admire the leaders (i.e. pope, patriarchs, bishops, priests, Dalai lama, etc) of other religions and perversions of Christianity. We sometimes seek to find the good in other religions because of their good works or zeal rather than remembering the truth of Jesus Christ that alone sets free from death and sin. I remember one person saying to me that Muslims are just as zealous as evangelical Christians. There is

---

[1] This false religion became known as theological Liberalism or Modernism. You can read more about this false religion, which is alive and well today, in many books, the best of which (in my opinion) being *"Christianity and Liberalism"* by J. Gresham Machen.

only one problem: One's zeal towards a cause does not save. Only Jesus saves.

If zeal or religious devotion saved or counted for merit with God, Baal's 450 prophets would have carried the day. I have never seen a minister of the gospel cut himself with knives and run all day out of zeal for Christ. Few Christians have prayed for hours straight, let alone run around in circles and jumped up and down from morning to night. But Baal's prophets did this. If religious zeal counted for something, then the true God would have responded favorably to Baal's prophets by sending fire on their sacrifice.

Instead, the fruit of their idolatry was their death. Not one of Baal's prophets escaped (v. 40).

Through their religion's history, artwork, writings, and elaborate architecture, leaders of false religions seek to persuade people to take their eyes off of the true God and to appreciate the false gods of this world. Liberal theologians in many leading academic institutions teach a Christianity that is difficult to distinguish from secular beliefs or universalism. It is no wonder then that many churches teach the same thing.

In His judgment on the prophets of Baal, God teaches us that He does not find good in false religions and their followers. He will destroy them. Where is Diana of the Ephesians today? Where are her followers? Where is mighty Dagon of the Philistines? What happened to the great gods of the Romans and the Greeks? They are gone - forgotten, extinct, destroyed. We should pray for the conversion of the lost, witness to them the pure, free, and unchanging gospel and grace of Jesus Christ, and call them to repent and believe; but we should never stand in admiration of their vain zeal and devotion.

The judgment of God can sometimes be difficult to reconcile with our understanding of God's mercy. I always find Psalm 136:16-21 very helpful. God's judgment of His enemies is mercy to God's people. With the destruction of these false prophets, God delivered the Israelites from those who had devoted their lives to leading others into idolatry. Jezebel was still alive at this time, but her power would be decreased and soon her day of judgment would come, for God's mercy endures forever!

Consider God's mercy today. He is showing the greatness of His judgment that we might find refuge in Him alone who delivers us from the judgment, even Jesus Christ our Lord and Savior. Many are the vain imaginations of the world when it comes to the Bible, Christianity, and other religions. None of those imaginations will stand on the great day of the Lord. Trust in the Lord Jesus Christ of the Scripture alone. Nothing else is worthy of our trust, for nothing and no one else made us or saves us from our sins.

20

The Lord's Blessing

Then Elijah said to Ahab, "Go up, eat and drink; for there is the sound of abundance of rain." So Ahab went up to eat and drink. And Elijah went up to the top of Carmel; then he bowed down on the ground, and put his face between his knees, and said to his servant, "Go up now, look toward the sea." So he went up and looked, and said, "There is nothing." And seven times he said, "Go again." Then it came to pass the seventh time, that he said, "There is a cloud, as small as a man's hand, rising out of the sea!" So he said, "Go up, say to Ahab, Prepare your chariot, and go down before the rain stops you." Now it happened in the meantime that the sky became black with clouds and wind, and there was a heavy rain. So Ahab rode away and went to Jezreel. Then the hand of the Lord came upon Elijah; and he girded up his loins and ran ahead of Ahab to the entrance of Jezreel.

I Kings 18:41-46 NKJV

Who is the fastest runner in history? Google will tell you it is Usain Bolt, who reached 27 mph. Those familiar with Mr. Bolt's performance will remember that he reached these speeds at race distances of 100 and 200 meters. Some horses have been clocked at over 50 mph and many race horses can sustain speeds well over 20 mph.

About 3,000 years ago, the hand of the Lord was on Elijah the prophet when he ran faster from Mount Carmel to Jezreel (about 20 miles) than the horses of King Ahab's Chariot. The skeptic would say the rain started and Ahab's chariot got stuck in the mud; the mention of the hand of the Lord upon Elijah reveals this was no mere natural phenomenon but a supernatural act of God.[1]

We first read of Elijah when he was sent to Ahab to tell him that God was withholding rain from the earth (17:1). Three years later, with the people starving and the land dry, the Lord showed His great power to Israel with fire on Mount Carmel. With that demonstration the Lord determined to send rain back to Israel (18:41).

After Elijah revealed God's will to Ahab regarding the rain he did something exemplary for all who follow after him in the faith: He went to the top of Mount Carmel and prayed.

How often do we give thanks, praise, and adoration to the Lord for the great works he has done for us in the past? We often pray asking God for needs in the present. We often pray asking for the fire from heaven. But how do we respond to God when He gives us those desires of our prayers and much more? God answered Elijah's prayer wonderfully and dreadfully. God destroyed the prophets of Baal. God protected Elijah those three years. God was sending rain again to Israel. So Elijah went to the top of the mountain and prayed. May we spend much time in prayer to the Lord thanking Him for His answers to prayer and pleading with Him for strength, faith, and perseverance for the trials that await us in the future.[2]

While Elijah was praying on the mountain he sent his servant seven times to search for the rain clouds over the Mediterranean Sea. It started with a little cloud on the seventh trip. From that

---

[1] Elijah's twenty mile run reminds me of Psalm 118: 29,31-33 *"For by you I can run against a troop, and by my God I can leap over a wall... For who is God, but the Lord? And who is a rock, except our God? The God who equipped me with strength and made my way blameless. He made my feet like the feet of a deer and set me secure on the heights."*

[2] It will not be a life of ease for Elijah from here on out. Queen Jezebel still has her mind set on Elijah's murder.

small cloud came a great rain fall, the likes of which the Israelites had not seen in at least three years. After God's judgment on His enemies, He literally poured out His showers of blessings on His people.

Each Sunday at my church (www.ropc.org) our pastor reminds us where our help comes from, *"My help comes from the Lord, who made the heaven and the earth"* (Psalm 121:2). Israel's help came from the Lord. Elijah's help came from the Lord. Where does your help come from today? May it always be from the Lord, for He alone *"will keep your going out and your coming in from this time forth and forevermore"* (Psalm 121:8).

As the rain was coming and Ahab was heading back to Jezreel the Lord put His hand on Elijah to run!

Eric Liddle is quoted as saying, *"God made me fast. And when I run, I feel His pleasure."* God made Elijah fast that day, and through the power of the Spirit that was upon Him, he probably felt and certainly knew God's pleasure!

21

The Irony of Idolaters

*And Ahab told Jezebel all that Elijah had done, also how he
had executed all the prophets with the sword. Then Jezebel sent a
messenger to Elijah, saying, "So let the gods do to me, and more
also, if I do not make your life as the life of one of them by
tomorrow about this time." And when he saw that, he arose and
ran for his life, and went to Beersheba, which belongs to Judah,
and left his servant there.*

I Kings 19:1-3 NKJV

R ecently my family ready Psalm 78. This chapter recounts
many wonderful works of the Lords: the plagues in Egypt
(vs. 43-52); the crossing of the Red Sea (vs. 13, 53); the
cloud to guide by day, the fire by night, the water from a rock,
manna and quail in the wilderness (vs. 14-29); the taking of
promised land (vs. 55); and the crowning of King David (vs. 70).
But throughout all of these accounts the Lord tells us things like
this, *"And they sinned yet more against Him...and they tempted
God...Yes, they spake against God...For all this they sinned
still..."* (vs. 17-19, 32).

The lesson is this, the revelation of the glorious works of the Lord
does not guarantee the salvation of sinners. For with all of these
great wonders the people still rebelled against God. Rather, it is
only those who hear, read, and see the works of the Lord and trust
in the Lord who works (vs. 7) who will be saved.

After Elijah beat Ahab to Jezreel, Ahab told his wife Jezebel all that
"Elijah" had done on Mount Carmel (19:1). We should notice that
Ahab does not tell what the "Lord" had done on Mount Carmel

but what "Elijah" had done. When Jezebel heard the report, especially that of the slain 450 prophets of her beloved god, she was filled with anger and made a vow to kill Elijah within 24 hours (19:2).

Jezebel's vow was quite revealing. She vowed by her gods.[1] Let her gods make her like one of the 450 prophets of Baal if Elijah was not killed with 24 hours. This vow should remind us of the vow made by certain Jews in Jerusalem to kill Paul (Acts 23:12). They would neither eat bread nor drink until they had killed Paul.

Such is the hatred of the wicked against the followers, especially the preachers, of the only living and true God. They will wish bodily harm on themselves rather than letting God's prophets to live. The irony with Jezebel was the gods she just swore by were the gods that could not answer 450 prophets on Mount Carmel. The man she just promised to murder was the man who stood up against her gods and the man whose God just defeated all of her prophets of Baal.

The wicked make ironic and sinful vows and they have no problem braking or contradicting them either. Elijah, upon receiving the message from Jezebel took his servant and fled to Beersheba, a famous city at the far southern end of Judah. It was well south of Jerusalem and under the control and protection of good King Jehoshaphat. Elijah left his servant in Beersheba so that the servant would be safe from Jezebel's assassins and so that Elijah might be alone for sometime with the Lord.

Christians are sometimes made to face evil and sometimes able to flee from it as was often the case in Elijah's life. By escaping, Elijah who just showed Ahab and all Israel that the gods of Jezebel were false gods, demonstrated this reality directly to Jezebel for her

---

[1] Most of the ancient idolaters were polytheists in that they had a multitude of gods. Jezebel loved Baal most but clearly by her name and background was content to worship many gods. ("Bel" was a Chaldean god.)

gods could not deliver Elijah's life into her hands. The Lord God again protected His servant Elijah for God had work for him to do.

Many great works of the Lord were seen by the Israelites in the wilderness and yet they spoke against God and died in the wilderness. Many great works were done in front of Ahab and Jezebel and they only became more hardened against the Lord. As we see the great works of the Lord here in I Kings may we hope in God, trust in God, and go about the work God has given us to do with another day of life on this Earth.

22

Elijah's Request

But he himself went a day's journey into the wilderness, and came and sat down under a broom tree. And he prayed that he might die, and said, "It is enough! Now, Lord, take my life, for I am no better than my fathers!" Then as he lay and slept under a broom tree, suddenly an angel touched him, and said to him, "Arise and eat." Then he looked, and there by his head was a cake baked on coals, and a jar of water. So he ate and drank, and lay down again. And the angel of the Lord came back the second time, and touched him, and said, "Arise and eat, because the journey is too great for you." So he arose, and ate and drank; and he went in the strength of that food forty days and forty nights as far as Horeb, the mountain of God.

I Kings 19:4-8 NKJV

"They made a calf in Horeb, and worshipped the molten image." Psalm 106:19

Where did the children of Israel make and worship a molten image? *"And it came to pass, as soon as he came nigh unto the camp, that he saw the calf, and the dancing: and Moses' anger waxed hot, and he cast the tables out of hands, and brake them beneath the mount" (Exodus 32:19).* The golden calf was made at the base of Mount Sinai while Israel was camped in Sinai from Exodus 19 until Numbers 10:12. Why then does the Psalmist refer to Horeb and what is the significance of Elijah's journey to Horeb? Horeb and Mt Sinai are two names in Scripture for the same place.

Elijah continued South from Beersheba out of the promised land and back into the same wilderness where the Israelites had wandered for 40 years because of their sin against the Lord. Like Hagar and Jonah, Elijah came to rest under a tree and requested death. *"It is enough; now, O Lord, take away my life; for I am not better than my fathers (19:4)."*

Does it sometimes seem to you that you have done the work the Lord has called you to and now it is time to depart from this world to the glory that awaits? Perhaps you feel you are at the end of your strength. Elijah the prophet certainly felt that way as he went to sleep under the Juniper tree to await God's answer to his request for death.

But like Moses at 80 years old and Zechariah well into old age, the Lord was not finished with His servant Elijah. So the Lord twice awoke Elijah by an angel and fed him food and water. From this heavenly food, Elijah was strengthened to travel 40 days and 40 nights, even all the way to the Southern end of the wilderness and unto the Mountain of God, Horeb, Mt. Sinai itself.

No doubt this food reminded Elijah and should remind us of the angels bread, even the manna that God gave His people in the wilderness. The water reminds us of the rock in the wilderness from where the water came out... and the rock was Christ. The number of days in the journey reminds us of the number of years of Israel's wandering. The reason for Elijah's time in the wilderness reminds us of the reasons for Israel's wandering, even the sin and idolatry of Israel. The destination of Elijah's wilderness journey reminds us of the presence of God, the voice of God, the law of God, that was given and revealed in that mountain (more to come on this).

God did not leave His people in the wilderness forever. He had work for them to do in Canaan and He preserved those 20 years and younger for 40 years to see and to show His glory to all the nations. So the Lord had work for Elijah to do and refreshing his servant at His mountain, He prepared him for that great work.

Where do you go when in need of refreshment? Where do you go when the work seems hard and you have done much already? Go to the Lord, the rock of your salvation, your help, and your God. He alone sustained Israel, He alone sustained Elijah, He alone will sustain you.

23

A Still Small Voice (Part 1)

*And there he went into a cave, and spent the night in that place;
and behold, the word of the Lord came to him, and He said to him,
"What are you doing here, Elijah?" So he said, "I have been
very zealous for the Lord God of hosts; for the children of Israel
have forsaken Your covenant, torn down Your altars, and killed
Your prophets with the sword. I alone am left; and they seek to
take my life." Then He said, "Go out, and stand on the mountain
before the Lord." And behold, the Lord passed by, and a great and
strong wind tore into the mountains and broke the rocks in pieces
before the Lord, but the Lord was not in the wind; and after the
wind an earthquake, but the Lord was not in the earthquake; and
after the earthquake a fire, but the Lord was not in the fire; and
after the fire a still small voice.*

I Kings 19:9-12 NKJV

Why do you suppose that as Jesus was transfigured on the high mountain in front of Peter, James, and John in Matthew 17, that standing next to him were Moses and Elijah? God the Father proclaimed His Son. In what way did Moses and Elijah bear witness?

It is difficult to read of Elijah's meeting with the Lord in these four verses of I Kings 19 without thinking of Moses' meeting with the Lord in Exodus 34.

In our text, Elijah was told to go and stand on the Mountain (19:11) and was there on that mountain in a cave (19:14). In Exodus 34, Moses was told to present himself to God at the top of Mount Sinai (34:2) and God would put him into a cave "cleft" of a rock (33:22). In Exodus, God passed by and revealed His name. In I Kings, the Lord passed by and spoke to His servant Elijah.

Moses was wearied from his labors with a stubborn people. Elijah was wearied from the stubbornness of Israel and the threats of Jezebel. In both instances the Lord would comfort His prophets by speaking to them.

"Why are you here?" Elijah was a long way from Israel. He wasn't even bordering Israel anymore but the entire country of Judah was between him and the nation he was called to serve. Elijah's answer was to defend his work. Perhaps, Elijah was trying to justify why he left his place of ministry in Israel. He left because he was jealous for the Lord. The children of Israel forsook God's covenant, broke apart his altars (Elijah rebuilt one of the Lord's altars on Mount Carmel that had previously been destroyed); and murdered God's prophets. So great had been the persecution, Elijah believed himself to be the only prophet left alive and Jezebel was hunting for him.

With this answer the Lord sent three great perils to Elijah on the mountain: a great wind; an earthquake; and fire. The Lord sent these things but the Lord was not speaking in any of these signs. Surely this should remind us of the devouring fire, earthquakes, and thunder (Ex. 19:16-18) which the Israelites witnessed upon their arrival to Mount Sinai. But the Lord did not speak to the Israelites through those great events, rather He spoke His words to His servant Moses who spoke them to the people. So with Elijah, the text says "but the Lord was not in the wind... earthquake... and fire."

These great manifestations of the power and might of the Lord were not the voice of the Lord that Elijah yearned for. The voice was yet to come: after the wind, the earthquake, and fire, "a still small voice" (19:12).

The Lord connected Elijah with Moses for us in a glorious way at Mount Sinai. The law represented by Moses and the prophets represented by Elijah are testifying to the person and work , power and might, glory and majesty of Jesus Christ. The Lord does not forget His people or His promises. He who showed His glory and holiness to Israel in the wilderness with the giving of the law at Mount Sinai was showing it again in Elijah's day and in these last days has revealed His glory through His Son and our Lord Jesus Christ.

Is it any wonder then that Moses and Elijah were with Jesus on the mount of Transfiguration? The Lord was connecting His covenant people through all ages.[1] They who were comforted by Christ on Mount Sinai, there stood as a testimony to the Father's Word that the promised Messiah is Jesus Christ who is faithful to His people today and forever. "Listen to Him!"

Moses and Elijah were comforted by the word of God on Mount Sinai. May the Lord comfort you with His Word today.

---

[1] For many years a great folly was taught in some churches and it seems to be alive and well in some places today: the Old Testament is not necessary or particularly helpful for Christians today. Some of the ministers of the largest churches in my home state teach this folly and the fruits of it in the lives of their members is spiritual disaster.

24

A Still Small Voice (Part 2)

And there he went into a cave, and spent the night in that place;
and behold, the word of the Lord came to him, and He said to him,
"What are you doing here, Elijah?" So he said, "I have been
very zealous for the Lord God of hosts; for the children of Israel
have forsaken Your covenant, torn down Your altars, and killed
Your prophets with the sword. I alone am left; and they seek to
take my life." Then He said, "Go out, and stand on the mountain
before the Lord." And behold, the Lord passed by, and a great and
strong wind tore into the mountains and broke the rocks in pieces
before the Lord, but the Lord was not in the wind; and after the
wind an earthquake, but the Lord was not in the earthquake; and
after the earthquake a fire, but the Lord was not in the fire; and
after the fire a still small voice.

I Kings 19:9-12 NKJV

What will satisfy your spiritual desires today? Do you look for a sign? Or do you look for something better?

One of Jesus' frequent rebukes in His earthly ministry was the desire for signs to be revealed. *"This is an evil generation: they seek a sign..."* (Luke 11:29). *"An evil and adulterous generation seeks after a sign...* (Matthew 12:39). The rich man wanted someone to return from the dead. The Pharisees and scribes tempted Christ for a sign. Even the devil desired Jesus to do a sign, *"command this stone that it be made bread"* (Luke 4:3). Instead, Jesus would give them the "sign of the prophet Jonah." Instead of a man returning from the dead, Jesus had given Moses and the Prophets. What was the sign of Jonah to Nineveh? "The preaching of Jonah" (Matthew 12:41).

The account of the voice of God speaking to Elijah is one that we should not pass over quickly. First came the great signs that the world wants to see and learn great truths from. A great wind, a great earthquake, a great fire. Surely these are the places, the wonders, that the world wants to hear the voice of God from. They forget the fear and dread of Israel at the base of Mount Sinai when they saw such things. But these are the things the world desires. Perhaps you and I have at times desired such wonderful signs from God to give meaning and insight into our lives. "But the Lord was not in the wind... the earthquake... [or] the fire" (I Kings 19:11).

The great signs of God tell us of His power and might. Coronavirus teaches us of the might of God and weakness of man. But none of these things tell us what we are to believe concerning God and what duty God requires of man. None of these signs teach us of the person of Jesus Christ and His great work for us as He lived a perfect life and died a shameful sinless death for sinners such as me. The great message of Christ crucified, dead, and risen is found only in the word of God, the Scriptures. *"...and after the fire a still small voice."*

Is the Bible enough for you? Does the Word of God satisfy the spiritual desires of your heart? If yes, feast on it, for man shall live by every word that proceeds from the mouth of God. *"How sweet are thy words unto my taste! yea, sweeter than honey to my mouth"* (Psalm 119:103). If no, have you considered that you may not yet know the true Christ? The Ninevites will rise up in judgment against the children of this age because they heard the preaching of Jonah, repented and believed in Jesus Christ the promised Messiah and were saved. If you will not believe Moses and the prophets, you will not believe even if a great sign is given to you like one rising from the dead. But, if you will listen to the voice of God as He speaks in His Word and by His Holy Spirit today, then you will know and believe in Him who saves and will be filled with the living water that will quench your thirst for spiritual things forevermore!

May we like Elijah listen to the voice of Jesus in His Word today. *"The Jews require a sign, and the Greeks seek after wisdom: But we preach Christ crucified, unto the Jews a stumbling block, and unto the Greeks foolishness; but unto them which are called, both Jews and Greeks, Christ the power of God, and the wisdom of God."* (I Cor. 1:22-23).

25

God Establishes Kingdoms

"So it was, when Elijah heard it, that he wrapped his face in his mantle and went out and stood in the entrance of the cave. Suddenly a voice came to him, and said, "What are you doing here, Elijah?" And he said, "I have been very zealous for the LORD God of hosts; because the children of Israel have forsaken Your covenant, torn down Your altars, and killed Your prophets with the sword. I alone am left; and they seek to take my life." Then the LORD said to him: "Go, return on your way to the Wilderness of Damascus; and when you arrive, anoint Hazael as king over Syria. Also you shall anoint Jehu the son of Nimshi as king over Israel. And Elisha the son of Shaphat of Abel Meholah you shall anoint as prophet in your place. It shall be that whoever escapes the sword of Hazael, Jehu will kill; and whoever escapes the sword of Jehu, Elisha will kill. Yet I have reserved seven thousand in Israel, all whose knees have not bowed to Baal, and every mouth that has not kissed him."

I Kings 19:13-18 NKJV

Sometimes prayers are answered far more wonderfully that we could have imagined. I confess that often I do not know what I need to pray for but the Lord Jesus Christ helps me to pray and intercedes for me and for all who believe in His name. When Elijah went to the Lord he requested that his life would be taken. He told the Lord of his zeal for the Lord's glory, the elimination of the Lord's prophets, and the wickedness of the king and queen of Israel.

Elijah was casting his cares on the Lord and laying his burdens at the feet of Him who carries us and our burdens. Some have criticized Elijah's comments as being too severe before the Lord and that the Lord was showing He was long suffering and gracious in His response so as to teach Elijah something Elijah was not appreciating at the moment. While we can agree the grace and mercy of the Lord was certainly on display (simply consider His gracious preservation of 7,000 and his merciful removal of a wicked royal line), we do not need to think poorly of Elijah's prayer and comments. The Lord did not rebuke or correct Elijah's prayers but rather seemed to confirm, acknowledge, and approve of Elijah's zeal as demonstrated in His answers to Elijah's prayer and reason for coming to Horeb. The Lord reminds us that He is jealous for His own name and glory and will not despise those who likewise are properly jealous for Him. After the demonstrations of the Lord's power and glory, He than directly answered Elijah.

First the Lord told of the means He would use to judge Israel (and Judah) for their sin. Elijah was told to anoint Hazael to be king over Syria to judge the populations of Israel and Judah. In the days of Elisha the prophet, Hazael brought much harm to Israel and Judah as the instrument of God's judgment on the land.[1]

Second the Lord told of the destruction of wicked Ahab, his wife, and the royal line of Israel. Elijah was called to anoint Jehu to be king of Israel in Ahab's place and the Lord promised to use Jehu to bring judgment on the house of Ahab.

Third, the Lord addressed Elijah's desire to depart from this world. In essence the Lord told Elijah that he was preparing for Elijah's entrance into glory by having Elijah call another prophet who would stand up in Elijah's place. With this promise came

---

[1] You can read of Hazael's conquest of Israel and Judah primarily in II Kings 12 though reference is made in other places including Amos 1

Scripture's first mention of the prophet who will have a double portion of Elijah's spirit, Elisha.[2]

Fourth, the Lord corrected Elijah's concerns about being the last Christian in Israel. As always, the Lord had his remnant of worshippers that would not bow down the knee to foolish idols. In Noah's day there were but eight souls. In Israel the number was nearly 1,000 times higher.

God will not be left without his remnant even in the worst of conditions. He is saving a people for Himself from every tribe, language, nation, and tongue. The wicked may try to wipe out Christ from their country, burn the Scriptures, and persecute His church, but God's people will remain even as they did in Israel, even if in small numbers.

Dear Christian, do not hesitate to cast your burdens and cares upon the Lord. He who carries us from the womb and continues to do so when we reach an old age and are wearing many gray hairs, will surely bear our burdens and will deliver us from them all. Go to Elijah's God and your God with humility, boldness, and confidence, as children to a Father, for He is able and ready to help us.

---

[2] I believe we can agree with Matthew Henry and Keil and Delitzsch that the reference to Elisha killing those escaping from Jehu's sword is a reference to killing with the sword of the Word of the Lord. While we might think of the incident with the children and the bears in II Kings 2, it was God who sent the bears at the word of Elisha and not Elisha's hand that killed the children. Furthermore in Jeremiah 1:10 and 18:7, the Word of the Lord from the prophet's mouth was used to tear down and destroy kingdoms. In this way we should take word figuratively even if at times God did use His prophets for the physical killing of God's enemies (i.e. Elijah orders the Israelites to kill the 450 prophets of Baal).

26

The Call of Elisha

So he departed from there, and found Elisha the son of Shaphat, who was plowing with twelve yoke of oxen before him, and he was with the twelfth. Then Elijah passed by him and threw his mantle on him. And he left the oxen and ran after Elijah, and said, "Please let me kiss my father and my mother, and then I will follow you." And he said to him, "Go back again, for what have I done to you?"

So Elisha turned back from him, and took a yoke of oxen and slaughtered them and boiled their flesh, using the oxen's equipment, and gave it to the people, and they ate. Then he arose and followed Elijah, and became his servant.

I Kings 19:19-21 NKJV

How do you respond to your calling from the Lord? Do you carry out the Lord's calling wholeheartedly without reservation or do you do so begrudgingly, wishing for something different?

When the Lord answered Elijah's prayer at Mt. Horeb (Sinai), the anointing of a prophet was third on the list. Nevertheless, it was the first action that took place after Elijah left Horeb. We do not know much about Elisha's life before he was called to be a prophet, but we can discern something from these verses.

Elisha was from a family of considerable means. He plowed with twelve yoke of oxen just after a terrible famine had been in the land for 3 years. He had sufficient oxen to kill some to give a feast for the family, servants, and perhaps neighbors. He lived in a good location in "the valley of dancing" (Abel-Meholah), which is believed to have been along the Jordan river and would have been one of the essential sources of sustenance during the famine. Elisha was a hard worker. He did not leave the work to the servants nor was he idle while waiting for a new vocation but he put all his efforts into the present calling God had given him: plowing the fields.

Elisha seemed already to be a follower of the Lord at the time Elijah threw him his mantle. He would almost certainly have been one of the 7,000 in Israel who had not bowed the knee to Baal (19:18). Elisha seemed to know who Elijah was and perhaps was at or near Mt. Carmel to observe the fire of the Lord and the victory over the prophets of Baal. He also seemed to be aware of the prophet's calling (throwing the mantle).

Elijah's mantle would take a very important place in Elisha's life in the coming chapters, but what we will focus on today is the willingness of Elisha to forsake mother, father, home, and wealth to follow the call of the Lord.[1] The call of a prophet was not a luxurious call nor a safe call. Israel was in rebellion against the Lord. Bounties were on the heads of the prophets. Many had already been killed, and many more would be killed. And yet, when the Lord called him through the prophet Elijah, he forsook all and followed the Lord.

We can be reminded here of Isaiah's calling in Isaiah 6 and of Jesus calling the disciples. Common men and noble men, fishermen, farmers, and tax collectors, they left their vocations immediately and followed the Lord. They carried out their callings through pain and suffering, sorrow and grief, for the rest of their lives, with most suffering terrible and cruel deaths as their entrance into glory.

---

[1] *"He who loves father or mother more than Me is not worthy of Me. And he who loves son or daughter more than Me is not worthy of Me. And he who does not take his cross and follow after Me is not worthy of Me. He who finds his life will lose it, and he who loses his life for My sake will find it."* (Matthew 10:37-39)

Elisha responded to his call by wrapping up his worldly affairs quickly. He said goodbye to his parents and had a farewell meal. Elijah recognized the great task ahead for Elisha and did not hinder him from this farewell.

After wrapping up his worldly affairs, Elisha followed Elijah and served him (19:21). He who had been a leader of men went and served the Lord's prophet. He who had put his hand to the plow would give his life to plow the fields of the world with the Word of God. He who harvested the grain would labor in the harvest of the Lord.

We have been given all varieties of callings. Some are more challenging than others. Some allow the living of comfortable lives while some require much sacrifice, difficulty, and pain. How will you carry out the calling God has called you to? If you are a stay-at-home mother, do you recognize the magnitude of your calling and do it with all your heart?[2] If you are an officer in the church, do you view your duties as a great responsibility from the Lord to be carried out with joy and much prayer? If you are a child, do you honor your parents and do your school work seeking to glorify God each day?

---

[2] It can be tempting for homemakers and mothers to view their lives and callings as less important than their husbands' callings and perhaps less important than the callings of other women who we see in the news. But who was it that taught Timothy the Word of God? Who was it that preserved Moses' life? Who was it that killed Sisera, a great enemy of the Lord, in her tent? Each day I go to work to earn income to support my family, my church, my country, etc. This is important, required by God, and I would be worse than an infidel if I did not provide for my own. But my wife is home teaching our children the ways of the Lord by instruction and example that will have lasting spiritual impact for many generations. Let us never look down on our callings that God has given us. If that is plowing fields, may we do it with all our might. If that is janitorial work, may we glorify God in that labor. If that is as the CEO of a company may we carry out that work for God's glory. In all that we do, single or married, student or laborer, old or young, may we do it all for the glory of God. (Colossians 3:17; I Cor 10:31).

God has called each of us to different tasks. Perhaps some day He will call us to other tasks. Only the Lord knows. Until the Lord calls us to glory may we pursue our callings with all the energy and zeal that we see from Elisha the prophet of God who put his might into his labors for the glory of the Lord.

27

The First Battle with Ben-Hadad

"Now Ben-Hadad the king of Syria gathered all his forces together; thirty-two kings were with him, with horses and chariots. And he went up and besieged Samaria, and made war against it. Then he sent messengers into the city to Ahab king of Israel, and said to him, "Thus says Ben-Hadad: 'Your silver and your gold are mine; your loveliest wives and children are mine.' " And the king of Israel answered and said, "My lord, O king, just as you say, I and all that I have are yours." Then the messengers came back and said, "Thus speaks Ben-Hadad, saying, 'Indeed I have sent to you, saying, "You shall deliver to me your silver and your gold, your wives and your children"; but I will send my servants to you tomorrow about this time, and they shall search your house and the houses of your servants. And it shall be, that whatever is pleasant in your eyes, they will put it in their hands and take it."

So the king of Israel called all the elders of the land, and said, "Notice, please, and see how this man seeks trouble, for he sent to me for my wives, my children, my silver, and my gold; and I did not deny him." And all the elders and all the people said to him, "Do not listen or consent." Therefore he said to the messengers of Ben-Hadad, "Tell my lord the king, All that you sent for to your servant the first time I will do, but this thing I cannot do." And the messengers departed and brought back word to him. Then Ben-Hadad sent to him and said, "The gods do so to me, and more also, if enough dust is left of Samaria for a handful for each of the people who follow me." So the king of Israel answered and said, "Tell him, Let not the one who puts on his armor boast like the one who takes it off."

And it happened when Ben-Hadad heard this message, as he and the kings were drinking at the command post, that he said to his servants, "Get ready." And they got ready to attack the city.

Suddenly a prophet approached Ahab king of Israel, saying, "Thus says the LORD: 'Have you seen all this great multitude? Behold, I will deliver it into your hand today, and you shall know that I am the LORD." So Ahab said, "By whom?" And he said, "Thus says the LORD: By the young leaders of the provinces." Then he said, "Who will set the battle in order?" And he answered, "You." Then he mustered the young leaders of the provinces, and there were two hundred and thirty-two; and after them he mustered all the people, all the children of Israel—seven thousand. So they went out at noon.

Meanwhile Ben-Hadad and the thirty-two kings helping him were getting drunk at the command post. The young leaders of the provinces went out first. And Ben-Hadad sent out a patrol, and they told him, saying, "Men are coming out of Samaria!" So he said, "If they have come out for peace, take them alive; and if they have come out for war, take them alive." Then these young leaders of the provinces went out of the city with the army which followed them. And each one killed his man; so the Syrians fled, and Israel pursued them; and Ben-Hadad the king of Syria escaped on a horse with the cavalry. Then the king of Israel went out and attacked the horses and chariots, and killed the Syrians with a great slaughter.

And the prophet came to the king of Israel and said to him, "Go, strengthen yourself; take note, and see what you should do, for in the spring of the year the king of Syria will come up against you." Then the servants of the king of Syria said to him, "Their gods are gods of the hills. Therefore they were stronger than we; but if we fight against them in the plain, surely we will be stronger than they. So do this thing: Dismiss the kings, each from his position, and put captains in their places; and you shall muster an army like the army that you have lost, horse for horse and chariot for chariot. Then we will fight against them in the plain; surely we will be stronger than they." And he listened to their voice and did so."

I Kings 20:1-25 NKJV

God works in mysterious ways, but the ways that He works are always for this end: His own glory! God has revealed Himself to all men, but we have suppressed the truth of God in unrighteousness. So God reveals Himself to us over and over that we might know that He is the Lord. In Exodus 6 Moses told the Israelites how God would deliver them and what God would do to the Egyptians. *"I will take you as My people, and I will be your God. Then you shall know that I am the Lord your God who brings you out from under the burdens of the Egyptians"* (Exodus 6:7).

In I Kings 20:1-25, we learn that Ahab was being bullied by Ben-Hadad king of Syria. Ahab was willing to give mighty Ben-Hadad almost everything he had to avoid war, but even Ahab could only be pushed so far (vs. 7 & 8). Ben-Hadad used Ahab's refusals of his demands to declare war on Israel and gathered thirty-two kings together to destroy Samaria.

With the great host gathered against Ahab, preparing to attack the city that very day, two things took place. First, Ben-Hadad and his kings were so confident of victory they were getting drunk rather than preparing for battle (vs. 12, 16). Second, a prophet of the Lord came to Ahab with news.

Building on the revelation of the Lord at Mt. Carmel, the prophet told Ahab that the Lord would deliver the Syrians into the hand of Ahab that very day. Why? So that Ahab would know that Jehovah was the Lord (vs. 13). The Lord extended His kindness to wayward Israel yet further. He had sent rain for Israel's sustenance and would give military victory over their enemies.

232 princes of Israel led 7,000 soldiers out against Ben-Hadad and his mighty host.[1] When they engaged with Syria, each of the 7,232 soldiers of Israel killed the first Syrian they encountered. This initial momentum, coupled with all of the kings being drunk and unable to coherently command, led to an immediate rout of the Syrian army. Ahab then engaged in the assault by attacking the cavalry of Syria and this victory turned into a great slaughter of the Syrian army (vs. 21).

Idolaters cannot understand the cause for their own defeat, for darkness has blinded their eyes. Ben-Hadad's servants presented this analysis of the battle: The Israelites' gods were gods of the hills so they won fighting in the hills near Samaria. If a battle could be fought in the plains, surely the gods of Israel would be of no benefit and Syria would win. This madness made sense to Ben-Hadad, who made preparations for the second battle with Ahab, which would be far worse than the first.

Why does God tell us over and over that He alone is Lord? Why is this whole series of devotionals titled from I Kings 18, "The Lord, He is God"? Because like the Israelites in Egypt and Ahab in Israel, so we are quick to forget it. We are very tempted to see the glory of God revealed, stiffen our necks and harden our hearts, and forget that He is God. So we need to be reminded over and over.

Let us learn from this passage the immeasurable grace and mercy of the Lord who not only reveals Himself to us as the Lord but also enables us to embrace Jesus Christ by faith.

---

[1] Some have speculated that the 7,000 mentioned here must be the 7,000 who had not bowed the knee to Baal. While the numbers are the same, that is where the overlap ends. Scripture does not suggest that the 232 princes were leading the believers in Israel into battle. The princes simply led 7,000 soldiers into battle against the Syrians.

28

The Second Battle of Ben-Hadad Run

So it was, in the spring of the year, that Ben-Hadad mustered the Syrians and went up to Aphek to fight against Israel. And the children of Israel were mustered and given provisions, and they went against them. Now the children of Israel encamped before them like two little flocks of goats, while the Syrians filled the countryside. Then a man of God came and spoke to the king of Israel, and said, "Thus says the LORD: 'Because the Syrians have said, "The LORD is God of the hills, but He is not God of the valleys," therefore I will deliver all this great multitude into your hand, and you shall know that I am the LORD."

And they encamped opposite each other for seven days. So it was that on the seventh day the battle was joined; and the children of Israel killed one hundred thousand foot soldiers of the Syrians in one day. But the rest fled to Aphek, into the city; then a wall fell on twenty-seven thousand of the men who were left.

And Ben-Hadad fled and went into the city, into an inner chamber. Then his servants said to him, "Look now, we have heard that the kings of the house of Israel are merciful kings. Please, let us put sackcloth around our waists and ropes around our heads, and go out to the king of Israel; perhaps he will spare your life." So they wore sackcloth around their waists and put ropes around their heads, and came to the king of Israel and said, "Your servant Ben-Hadad says, 'Please let me live.' " And he said, " Is he still alive? He is my brother."

Now the men were watching closely to see whether any sign of mercy would come from him; and they quickly grasped at this word and said, "Your brother Ben-Hadad." So he said, "Go, bring him." Then Ben-Hadad came out to him; and he had him come up into the chariot. So Ben-Hadad said to him, "The cities which my

father took from your father I will restore; and you may set up
marketplaces for yourself in Damascus, as my father did in
Samaria." Then Ahab said, "I will send you away with this treaty."
So he made a treaty with him and sent him away.

I Kings 20:26-34 NKJV

I n 2009 the Manhattan Declaration was produced defending the
life of the unborn, religious freedom, and marriage. Some
Christians were quite upset at the number of Reformed
ministers who would not sign the declaration; ignoring the facts
that the declaration aligned Roman Catholics, Eastern Orthodox,
and evangelicals under the same faith and practice; that it
elevated human reason and nature to the same level of truth as
the Scripture; and that evangelicals have historically viewed
Roman Catholicism and the Orthodox religion as different religions
from evangelical Christianity. Many simply saw the goals of the
letter and ignored the preamble and much of the body. By signing
Christians agreed with some good statements but also some
statements that opposed God and His word.

As Ahab secured a great second victory over Ben-Hadad he would
do a similar thing. Desiring the cities and friendship offered by
Ben-Hadad, he would treat Ben-Hadad as a friend and call him
"brother," while ignoring Ben-Hadad's hatred of the true God,
God's express desire for Ben-Hadad's destruction, and the harm
done to His country by Ben-Hadad.

We can know with great certainty that an army was large when
God says their pack animals were without number and the host
was as the sand of the seashore. This was the description used by
God to describe the Midianites in Judges 7. God then used 300
men with Gideon to destroy them all.

The description in our text today is not much different. Israel's
army was like "two flocks of goats" while the Syrian army "filled
the countryside". From the world's perspective this match was

unfair and the result obvious: Syria would swallow Israel up. But the world would not understand the fatal flaw that Syria had made. They had spoken against the Lord, claiming He was only a god of the hills and not god of the plains. Now He who set the hills in their order and laid out the plains in their fashion had set His hand against them.

The second battle with Ben-Hadad made the first battle look like a skirmish. The Israelites killed 100,000 Syrians on the first day the battle was engaged. The Syrian army fled to Aphek and made a determined stand on and behind its defensive wall, hoping to hold the Israelites from further gains. Instead the Lord caused the wall to collapse and fall killing 27,000 additional soldiers. Surely now Ahab would know that the Lord was God alone (vs. 28) and finish off the wicked Syrian king.

At the destruction of his army, Ben-Hadad hid in the city. His servants persuaded him to present himself to Ahab in humble fashion and to seek his mercy. His servants begged Ahab for their king's life to be spared and Ahab responded in a manner that ought to widen the eyes of the reader: "Is he still alive? He is my brother" (vs. 32).

He who had harmed Israel for many years and mocked God was now called a brother, a close friend, by king Ahab. Ben-Hadad's clever servants caught onto this language and confirmed that Ben-Hadad was Ahab's brother. Ahab then took Ben-Hadad into his chariot and made a peace treaty with the king who had made war on the God of Israel.

We should not make friends with those who oppose the Lord Jesus Christ. Witness to them, do good to them, pray for them, but do not align yourself with their evil ways. II John 9-11 says of him who comes to you without the biblical doctrine of the Father and the Son, "do not receive him into your house nor greet him; for he who greets him shares in his evil deeds" (II John 11).

If we join with those who are against the true and living God we share in acting against God. Let us abide in the Lord, "that when He appears, we may have confidence and not be ashamed before Him at His coming" (I John 2:28).

29

Ahab for Ben-Hadad

Now a certain man of the sons of the prophets said to his neighbor by the word of the LORD, "Strike me, please." And the man refused to strike him. Then he said to him, "Because you have not obeyed the voice of the LORD, surely, as soon as you depart from me, a lion shall kill you." And as soon as he left him, a lion found him and killed him. And he found another man, and said, "Strike me, please." So the man struck him, inflicting a wound. Then the prophet departed and waited for the king by the road, and disguised himself with a bandage over his eyes.

Now as the king passed by, he cried out to the king and said, "Your servant went out into the midst of the battle; and there, a man came over and brought a man to me, and said, 'Guard this man; if by any means he is missing, your life shall be for his life, or else you shall pay a talent of silver.' While your servant was busy here and there, he was gone." Then the king of Israel said to him, "So shall your judgment be; you yourself have decided it. "

And he hastened to take the bandage away from his eyes; and the king of Israel recognized him as one of the prophets. Then he said to him, "Thus says the LORD: 'Because you have let slip out of your hand a man whom I appointed to utter destruction, therefore your life shall go for his life, and your people for his people.' " So the king of Israel went to his house sullen and displeased, and came to Samaria."

I Kings 20:35-43 NKJV

R ecently during an worship service we sang these lines from the hymn, "Lord with Glowing Heart I'd Praise Thee":

Praise the grace whose threats alarmed thee,
Roused thee from thy fatal ease;
Praise the grace whose promise warmed thee,
Praise the grace that whispered peace

Have you thought recently about the alarming warnings of the Lord against our fatal disobedience to the Word of the Lord? Have you considered God's grace to warn us from sin?

In the closing verses of I Kings 20, a prophet was sent to rebuke Ahab for allowing the enemy of God to remain alive. The rebuke is quite strong. Ben-Hadad was appointed by God for destruction and Ahab sinned against God by allowing him to live. The implication is that Ahab knew his job with Ben-Hadad and sinned against God by allowing him to live. He added to his mockery of God by calling Ben-Hadad his brother.

The prophet used a story and his own wound to demonstrate God's just anger towards Ahab who with his own mouth acknowledged the sin of his ways. I am reminded of the prophet Nathan's story to David, which was similar except that David repented at the prophet's words, while Ahab's heart was hard and he went back to Samaria displeased after his great victory.

Before all of these events took place, however, a very interesting account is given of the prophet and another man that requires our attention. The prophet spoke to his neighbor by the Word of the Lord with instruction, "Strike me, please." This was not an ordinary request, but it came from the Lord Himself. It was a great test for this other man like the tests of the Lord to Abraham to offer his only son Isaac or Noah to build an ark. The man was called by God to wound the prophet so that the prophet could teach King Ahab of his great sin.

"And the man refused to strike him" (vs. 35). God had given this man an extraordinary call, to strike the prophet. The man knew it was the Word of the Lord that called him to do it. And this man knowingly sinned against the Word of God. The result was the immediate discipline and judgment of the Lord, for a lion met him shortly after he departed from the prophet and killed him.

This account should rouse our senses and stir us from our easy going approach to the Scripture and commandments of the Lord. We should recognize the concern the Lord has for obedience to His Word. Disobeying God's Word is disobeying God Himself and worthy of death. Consider the cross of Christ. There we see our Savior bled and died for nothing He had done but for all the sins that we had committed which deserved death. Jesus Christ "became sin for us, He who knew no sin, that we might be made the righteousness of God in Him" (II Cor. 5:21).

Because Ahab let Ben-Hadad go, the Lord required Ahab's life in the place of Ben-Hadad's life. Because of our sins we deserve death. Because of the great love that God had for His own people, He sent His own Son, even our Lord Jesus Christ to suffer and die in our place. What wondrous love is this?

30

Naboth's Vineyard

And it came to pass after these things that Naboth the Jezreelite had a vineyard which was in Jezreel, next to the palace of Ahab king of Samaria. So Ahab spoke to Naboth, saying, "Give me your vineyard, that I may have it for a vegetable garden, because it is near, next to my house; and for it I will give you a vineyard better than it. Or, if it seems good to you, I will give you its worth in money." But Naboth said to Ahab, "The LORD forbid that I should give the inheritance of my fathers to you!" So Ahab went into his house sullen and displeased because of the word which Naboth the Jezreelite had spoken to him; for he had said, "I will not give you the inheritance of my fathers." And he lay down on his bed, and turned away his face, and would eat no food. But Jezebel his wife came to him, and said to him, "Why is your spirit so sullen that you eat no food?" He said to her, "Because I spoke to Naboth the Jezreelite, and said to him, 'Give me your vineyard for money; or else, if it pleases you, I will give you another vineyard for it. And he answered, 'I will not give you my vineyard." Then Jezebel his wife said to him, "You now exercise authority over Israel! Arise, eat food, and let your heart be cheerful; I will give you the vineyard of Naboth the Jezreelite."

And she wrote letters in Ahab's name, sealed them with his seal, and sent the letters to the elders and the nobles who were dwelling in the city with Naboth. She wrote in the letters, saying, Proclaim a fast, and seat Naboth with high honor among the people; and seat two men, scoundrels, before him to bear witness against him, saying, "You have blasphemed God and the king." Then take him out, and stone him, that he may die. So the men of his city, the elders and nobles who were inhabitants of his city, did as Jezebel had sent to them, as it was written in the letters which she had sent to them. They proclaimed a fast, and seated Naboth with high honor among the people. And two men, scoundrels, came in and sat before him; and the scoundrels witnessed against him, against Naboth, in the presence of the people, saying, "Naboth has blasphemed God and the king!" Then they took him outside the city and stoned him with stones, so that he died. Then they sent to Jezebel, saying, "Naboth has been stoned and is dead."

And it came to pass, when Jezebel heard that Naboth had been stoned and was dead, that Jezebel said to Ahab, "Arise, take possession of the vineyard of Naboth the Jezreelite, which he refused to give you for money; for Naboth is not alive, but dead." So it was, when Ahab heard that Naboth was dead, that Ahab got up and went down to take possession of the vineyard of Naboth the Jezreelite.

I Kings 21:1-16 NKJV

What do you learn from accounts of terrible sin like David's sin with Bathsheba; Cain and Abel; and Naboth and Ahab? There are at least two common elements these all share: 1) The nature of sin; and 2) The call to faithfulness.

"But each one is tempted when he is drawn away by his own desires and enticed. Then, when desire has conceived, it gives birth to sin; and sin, when it is full-grown, brings forth death." James 1:14-15

Ahab's discontent and envy led to complaining, complaining led to Jezebel's wicked plan, Jezebel's wicked plan led to lies, lies led to murder, and murder led to theft. Sin breeds sin.

Sin rarely ever occurs in isolation but like an avalanche it grows, expands, and devours many in its path. In Adam's fall, we sinned all. From Ahab's complaining spirit in front of his wife come the murder of Naboth and the theft of his property.

One of the lessons we should learn from Ahab's sin is to cut down our sin wherever we see it appear. If we are complaining, may we stop and give thanks to the Lord from whom all blessings flow. Let us "rejoice always" and "in everything give thanks." If our hearts' desire is on that which God has forbidden, whether that be the lusts of the flesh, the lust of the eyes, or the pride of life, may we humble ourselves before the Lord, be content with our lot, and flee from all that would cause us to fall. May we lift our eyes to Heaven from where comes our help and cry out, "Lead me not into temptation but deliver me from evil."

As far as we can tell, Ahab made Naboth a fair if not advantageous offer for his property. He would either give Naboth the market value for his vineyard or give to him a vineyard somewhere else better than his own. As reasonable as this might seem, there was one problem, God had forbidden the selling of the Israelites' inheritance (vs. 3).[1]

Ahab desired for Naboth to do something that was directly contrary to the Word of God. Because Naboth feared God more than man he would not consent. This decision by Naboth eventually cost him his life. It may have robbed a wife of her husband, and children of their father.

Following and serving Christ may come at great cost. Many have given their lives, lost their lives, and suffered great persecution for following Christ. Naboth was no fool. He knew of the wickedness of his royal neighbors. He knew of the murder of the prophets. He knew of the death warrant out for Elijah. And yet he would not sin against his God who sent fire from Heaven on Mt. Carmel.

---

[1] "So the inheritance of the children of Israel shall not change hands from tribe to tribe, for every one of the children of Israel shall keep the inheritance of the tribe of his fathers." (Numbers 36:7)

To fulfill all righteousness Jesus Christ was faithful even to His death on the cross. May we be faithful to the Lord our God even if it costs us everything. The losses of this world are nothing to be compared to the gains of the world to come. But if we sin against God and refuse to repent and turn to Him in faith, whatever gain we think we can receive in this life will provide no satisfaction or joy, and in the life to come we will have eternal death.

Through this account of Naboth, Ahab, and Jezebel, life and death are presented before you. Life in Jesus Christ. Death in sin and unrighteousness. Choose Life![2]

---

[2] "I announce to you today that you shall surely perish; you shall not prolong your days in the land which you cross over the Jordan to go in and possess. I call heaven and earth as witnesses today against you, that I have set before you life and death, blessing and cursing; therefore choose life, that both you and your descendants may live; that you may love the Lord your God, that you may obey His voice, and that you may cling to Him, for He is your life and the length of your days..." (Deut. 30: 18-20)

31

Selling Out To Evil

Then the word of the Lord came to Elijah the Tishbite, saying, "Arise, go down to meet Ahab king of Israel, who lives in Samaria. There he is, in the vineyard of Naboth, where he has gone down to take possession of it. You shall speak to him, saying, Thus says the Lord: "Have you murdered and also taken possession?" And you shall speak to him, saying, Thus says the Lord: "In the place where dogs licked the blood of Naboth, dogs shall lick your blood, even yours."

So Ahab said to Elijah, "Have you found me, O my enemy?" And he answered, "I have found you, because you have sold yourself to do evil in the sight of the Lord: Behold, I will bring calamity on you. I will take away your posterity, and will cut off from Ahab every male in Israel, both bond and free. I will make your house like the house of Jeroboam the son of Nebat, and like the house of Baasha the son of Ahijah, because of the provocation with which you have provoked Me to anger, and made Israel sin. And concerning Jezebel the Lord also spoke, saying, The dogs shall eat Jezebel by the wall of Jezreel. The dogs shall eat whoever belongs to Ahab and dies in the city, and the birds of the air shall eat whoever dies in the field. But there was no one like Ahab who sold himself to do wickedness in the sight of the LORD, because Jezebel his wife stirred him up. And he behaved very abominably in following idols, according to all that the Amorites had done, whom the LORD had cast out before the children of Israel."

I Kings 21:17-26 NKJV

How are you known by others today? How will you be remembered at your death? How does the Lord know you right now? Ahab who sinned against God more than any of the wicked kings of Israel before him is remembered for this: he sold himself to do evil in the sight of the Lord (vs. 20 and 25). Some people "sell out" for money or other reward. A traitor will sell secrets of his own country for money or promises of security from another country. Many will compromise morals and principles in exchange for financial reward. Ahab sold himself for this purpose: to do evil.

Naboth's blood cried out before the Lord, who sent His servant Elijah to condemn Ahab's sins. Jezebel hatched the plan against Naboth, but it was Ahab who initiated it with his complaining, allowed it to take place, and took the rewards of Jezebel's treachery. While Ahab was taking possession of the vineyard, the Lord sent Elijah.

Once again, before Ahab could enjoy his sin and wickedness, the Lord's condemnation weighed heavily on him. After the second battle of Ben-Hadad and the great victory of Israel over Syria, Ahab went home heavy of heart because of the prophecy of the Lord against him. So again, when Ahab went to take the fruits of his wickedness, the Lord sent His prophet to give Ahab the worst news of his life.

When he met Elijah before Mt. Carmel, Ahab lied in calling Elijah the "troubler of Israel" (18:17). When he met Elijah outside of the vineyard, Ahab did not lie but truthfully called Elijah his "enemy" (21:20). Ahab set himself against the Lord, which set Ahab against the Lord's prophet. Those who set themselves against the Lord set themselves against the Lord's people. Christians may fall into great harm if they reject that the world hates the Christian because it hates God. Do not seek friendship with the world but rather seek the salvation of the world.

The message of the Lord to Ahab was quite terrible. Ahab's family line would be cut off from the earth just like wicked kings Jeroboam and Baasha. It would be a terrible destruction because Ahab and Jezebel did not sin alone but caused all Israel to sin. The death of Ahab and Jezebel would be violent, and dogs would lick their blood just as dogs licked the blood of righteous Naboth who was executed as a blasphemer.

Never had there been someone who had sold himself to wickedness like Ahab. Never had a wife stirred up a husband to wickedness like Jezebel. Great would be the punishment of the Lord.

If we think of sin lightly we have erred greatly. The Lord is against those who are against Him and His holy ways. We must set our hearts, souls, strength, and mind to loving the Lord. How can you love the Lord? Keep His commandments. They are good. They teach you about Christ and His righteous ways, works, and word. Perhaps today you are known by others for sin. Even today, repent of your sins, believe in Jesus Christ, and be saved. If you are walking with the Lord, thank and praise the Lord. Give yourself over to following Him as He has revealed in His Word. And when your days draw to a close, the Lord will say to you, "Well done thou good and faithful servant."

32

Ahab's Humiliation

So it was, when Ahab heard those words, that he tore his clothes and put sackcloth on his body, and fasted and lay in sackcloth, and went about mourning. And the word of the Lord came to Elijah the Tishbite, saying, "See how Ahab has humbled himself before Me? Because he has humbled himself before Me, I will not bring the calamity in his days. In the days of his son I will bring the calamity on his house."

I Kings 21:27-29 NKJV

In Matthew 27:1-5, Judas acknowledged his sin, threw away the blood money for which he had betrayed Christ and committed suicide. The sorrow of the wicked is an outward sorrow for what has been done and its consequences on life. However, it is not repentance unto life.[1] It is not a remorse from the heart but outward remorse only.

We see this in children often and ourselves also if we are honest. A child caught stealing will often break down in tears. While this may be a godly, often times it is simply the response to being caught in an act of willful sin; the child now regrets it but would have been well satisfied with if he had not been caught.

When Ahab heard the condemnation of his sin and the judgment coming soon on his whole bloodline, he put on all the outward elements of repentance: fasting, sackcloth, mourning. None of

---

[1] Repentance unto life is a saving grace whereby a sinner out of a true sense of his sin and apprehension of the mercy of God in Christ does with grief and hatred of his sin turn from it unto God with full purpose of, and endeavor after, new obedience (Westminster Shorter Catechism answer #87).

these outward elements mean someone is actually repenting from his heart and unto the Lord. The Lord sees and knows nevertheless, the Lord showed His mercy temporarily, in accordance with Ahab's superficial repentance.

Many people in our day show the same sorrow as Ahab. We are tempted to repent and be sorrowful because someone caught us in our sin and we knew we shouldn't have done it. So we put on the appearance of repentance. We read the Bible more. We go to church more. We talk about praying more. All of these things are good, and this is not meant to disparage such activities but rather to say if all of those things are merely outward changes and not a response to the inward change of the penitent heart, then they are of no benefit to us.

When we come to the Lord like the publican and cry out to the Lord for mercy on us as sinners we recognize that we are unworthy of God's mercy, filled with sin and unrighteousness, and have our only hope of salvation in Christ alone who is merciful. It is the hour of salvation, and the Word is crying out, repent!

In his commentary on I Kings, Matthew Henry summarizes this picture of the Lord and Ahab beautifully in these words: "This encourages all those that truly repent and unfeignedly believe the holy gospel. If a pretending partial penitent shall go to his house reprieved, doubtless a sincere penitent shall go to his house justified."

33

What Communion Has Light With Darkness?

Now three years passed without war between Syria and Israel. Then it came to pass, in the third year, that Jehoshaphat the king of Judah went down to visit the king of Israel. And the king of Israel said to his servants, "Do you know that Ramoth in Gilead is ours, but we hesitate to take it out of the hand of the king of Syria? So he said to Jehoshaphat, Will you go with me to fight at Ramoth Gilead?

I Kings 22:1-4 NKJV

What comes to mind when you think of Jehoshaphat, King of Judah? Perhaps you remember that he was a good king. He "walked in the former ways of his father David; he did not seek the Baals" (2 Chron. 17:3). Perhaps you remember that the Lord established Judah under his rule because he feared the Lord and walked in His ways. Perhaps you remember that he removed the high places and idols from throughout the land. Perhaps you remember his great victory over Ammon, Moab, and Mount Seir in II Chronicles 20 when Jehoshaphat sent the singers in front of the army singing "Praise the LORD, for His mercy endures forever" (20:21).

There are many good things we should remember about Jehoshaphat, but there were also weaknesses and sins. The overarching sin of Jehoshaphat's reign in Judah was his alliances with the wicked kings of Israel. He allied himself both with Ahab as we see in II Kings 22 today as well as with Ahab's son Ahaziah (II Chron. 20:35). With Ahab in particular, Jehoshaphat joined himself through marriage by marrying Ahab's sister. The hearts of the people of Judah were never with the God of Jehoshaphat and perhaps this example with Israel was part of the reason.

The Lord gave peace to Ahab for three years after he let Ben-Hadad escape unharmed. Now the treaty had been broken, all the cities were not returned, and the enemy of God was on the doorstep of Israel. At this time Jehoshaphat came to visit, and Ahab invited Judah to fight Syria with Israel. In light of the life of Ahab and the righteousness of Jehoshaphat, the answer Jehoshaphat gave to Ahab is hard to believe: "Jehoshaphat said to the King of Israel, "I am as you are, my people as your people, my horses as your horses" (Vs. 4).

This unholy alliance brought shame on the name of the Lord. The alliance would nearly cost Jehoshaphat his life.

There is a temptation for God's people to desire acceptance by the world. Christian youth often feel like they are missing out on something by not being like the world. Christian adults will often make friendships with the world, even becoming unequally yoked by marrying unbelievers. The Lord warns us to avoid these alliances for the protection of our lives and our souls. "Ye adulterers and adulteresses, know ye not that the friendship of the world is enmity with God? whosoever therefore will be a friend of the world is the enemy of God" (James 4:4).

Ahab was an enemy of God. Jehoshaphat was a friend of God. What fellowship has light with darkness? There is none. They are opposites. They are opposed. "God is light and in Him is no darkness at all. If we say that we have fellowship with Him, and walk in darkness, we lie and do not practice the truth" (I John 1:5-6).

Dear Christian, the world entices us in many ways. Many have been like Ahab and sold themselves to the evils of the world. Many Christians have pursued friendship with the world and temporarily have made themselves out to be enemies of God. Such behavior will only lead to the discipline of a Heavenly Father. When we meet Jehoshaphat in Heaven we can ask him about his life and what he was thinking while aligning with the king worse than all others before him. But while on earth let us learn to avoid evil fellowship and to "cast off the works of darkness, and let us put on the armor of light. Let us walk properly, as in the day, not in revelry and drunkenness, not in lowness and lust, not in strife and envy. But put on the LORD Jesus Christ, and make no provision for the flesh, to fulfill its lusts" (Romans 13:12-14).

34

False Teachers Part 1: The Desire for a Word From The LORD

Also Jehoshaphat said to the king of Israel, "Please inquire for the word of the LORD today."

I Kings 22:5 *NKJV*

If you desire to know the will of the Lord on a particular matter, where will you go to find it? You can type the question into Google and have hundreds of websites giving you an answer. You can listen to sermons by dozens of pastors on the very topic you wish to know about. The resources on spiritual things are innumerable. The only problem is many of these resources and teachers will not tell you the truth.

Many of those listening to and supporting these teachers don't want to hear the truth but desire to be told fables. Like good marketers, the false prophets, pastors, and teachers give their hearers what they want to hear and in so doing they reap the worldly rewards of wealth, fame, and power.

"For the time will come when they will not endure sound doctrine, but according to their own desires, because they have itching ears, they will heap up for themselves teachers; and they will turn their ears away from the truth, and be turned aside to fables." II Timothy 4:3-4

Occasionally I will listen to 'sermons' from televangelists and celebrity pastors, some of whom can secure millions of listeners to a single week's sermon while a respected Reformed pastor can top out at fewer than 1,000 clicks. Many celebrity pastors will flatter with their lips, telling people everything good they want to hear about themselves and their future, particularly related to health, wealth, and prosperity. They sprinkle in a half dozen Bible references to make the message sound biblical and leave people worse than where they began. While they may cite a verse about repentance and the work of Christ, they are unlikely to call people to repent of their sins, flee from the wrath of God to come, and believe in the Lord Jesus Christ alone for salvation.

All people want to hear a word from their god. The Christian seeks to know the Word of the true God and ought to give ear only to those pastors and teachers who give people a sense for the meaning of the Scripture. The unbeliever deludes himself into thinking the lies he wants to hear about his god are the actual Word of the true God. In both cases, there is a desire for knowledge and understanding from God but only one source contains the truth.

Although Jehoshaphat foolishly went to Israel and made an alliance with Ahab to fight against Syria, he also made a wise decision: to seek the will of the Lord (vs. 5). We too should seek the will of the Lord in all things. Are we thinking and acting in accordance with Scripture or after our own deceitful lusts? We have been given the mind of Christ in the Word, and we should seek after Him where and while He may be found.

The events that transpired after Jehoshaphat's request teach us many things about false prophets and teachers. May the Lord use this portion of Scripture to help us protect, proclaim, and promote the truth of the Lord Jesus Christ to a dead, dying, and delusional world.

35

False Teachers Part 2: Their Numbers

Then the king of Israel gathered the prophets together, about four hundred men, and said to them, "Shall I go against Ramoth Gilead to fight, or shall I refrain?" So they said, "Go up, for the Lord will deliver it into the hand of the king."

I Kings 22:6 *NKJV*

There is a road near our church that our family calls False Religion Freeway. It starts with a large Hindu temple, one of the most elaborate sites in the world and filled with more ornaments and idols than most other buildings in North America. After you drive past the gated temple and make a left you will pass a World Mission Society Church of God building. This cult believes in god the father and god the mother who came in the flesh in South Korea. Blocks away is a Jehovah's Witness Kingdom Hall where Jesus Christ's deity is denied and millions are being led to destruction through the false teaching of a few false prophets in the secretive Watchtower. Just after our own church comes a large Roman Catholic Church where Jesus Christ is said to be sacrificed over and over by "priests" in the mass each day. All around our homes and churches are false teachings, false religions, and perversions of the Word of God. It is sometimes discouraging to see so many deceivers so close together.

When Jehoshaphat asked for the Word of God to be proclaimed, 400 false "prophets of the Lord" were immediately made available. King Ahab had 400 false prophets as part of his retinue. Given that Israel's army was relatively small in comparison to neighboring countries like Syria, the number dedicated to prophecy is all the more staggering.

Some have tied the 400 prophets in I Kings 22 to the 400 prophets of Ashteroth (of the groves) in I Kings 18:19. Many Bibles cross reference to these two verses. The numbers are the same but there seems to be disagreement over whether or not these are the same 400 prophets. One of two scenarios seems to me to be the case: 1) The prophets of Ashteroth became false prophets of the Lord after the defeat of the prophets of Baal at Mt. Carmel; or 2) These were simply 400 men who claimed to be prophets of the Lord with no relation to the prophets of Ashteroth. I find the second scenario more in line with the text.

The lesson is this: False prophets and teachers are numerous. There is a huge demand by the world for these false teachers because ears itch to hear a false word of the Lord. We need to guard ourselves from them lest we fall under the spell of their fables.

How can we guard ourselves against false prophets and teachers? Know the truth! Know God's Word so well through reading it and listening to faithful preaching that any false presentation puts you on alert and guard. Know the Lord Jesus Christ so well that counterfeits are easy to fake. I suspect married couples could easily spot a fake spouse who came into their home. Our King, Lord, and God has revealed Himself to us through 66 books of the Scripture. Shouldn't we know Him well enough to spot and reject frauds?

Jehoshaphat recognized immediately that the 400 were not true prophets of the Lord (vs. 6). May the Lord Jesus Christ guard our hearts, minds, and souls from the false prophets filling the highways and byways around us.

36

False Teachers Part 3: Their Message

Then the king of Israel gathered the prophets together, about four hundred men, and said to them, "Shall I go against Ramoth Gilead to fight, or shall I refrain?" So they said, "Go up, for the Lord will deliver it into the hand of the king.

I Kings 22:6 NKJV

W ould you like to find God's secret cure for the COVID-19 virus? There are prophets out there just waiting to sell you the cure. What about a 2020 understanding of end times prophecies? How about learning the effects of a recent setback on your future? So called apostles and prophets are standing by to explain how that "setback is just a setup" for better things.[1] Whatever you want to hear about, whatever you want to be told, a 'prophet,' 'teacher,' or 'apostle' of the Lord is standing by to give you his message... in exchange for a small donation to the ministry.

False prophets have a common *modus operandi* - they tell their followers what they want to hear. Jim Jones's followers wanted signs and wonders so he made elaborate hoaxes to convince followers those signs were happening. Followers of the World

---

[1] One of Joel Osteen's regular phrases in 2020 is that your setback is just a setup for greater things. He uses Joseph's imprisonment, David on the run from Saul, and other biblical stories to prove this to you. He does not speak in an ultimate sense of Heaven for those who are in Christ but in a worldly sense, focusing on the present here and now. In the world we will have tribulation, we will suffer a little while, but Joel Osteen ignores all that and promises a great life now and in the near future. People want to hear this, want to believe it, want to experience it, and so they keep on listening to this great flatterer.

Mission Society Church of God want to hear about a female mother god and so they are given one... in the flesh even as a bonus (just don't ask how god the father could have died). Followers of Harold Camping wanted to hear a date for the return of Christ in their lifetime and they received it.

Ahab wanted to go up to Ramoth Gilead to fight against the Syrians so his 400 false prophets told him exactly what he wanted to hear: "Go up for the Lord will deliver it into the hand of the King" (vs. 6). These prophets claimed to speak in the name of the Lord Jehovah. They presented their message as if it came from God Himself, and the message was precisely what Ahab wanted Jehoshaphat and himself to hear. But the message was false. These prophets were fake perhaps the 400 even deceived themselves as they deceived Ahab.

"For there shall arise false Christs, and false prophets, and shall show great signs and wonders; insomuch that, if it were possible, they shall deceive the very elect" (Matthew 24:24).

Be on guard against those who flatter you by telling you all you want to hear. The Word of the Lord will do many profitable things for us: convict and rebuke us of our sin; correct us when we err in our thoughts and ways; give to us sound doctrine about our Triune God and what we are to believe concerning Him; instruct us in how we are to live our lives before our Holy God; and set our minds on things above; but it will not flatter us with lies.[2]

When the Bereans heard the Word preached from the Apostle Paul in Acts 17:11-12, they searched the Scripture to see if those things were true. When we hear and read teachers let us search the Scriptures to see if such messages are from the Word of God. Pray for wisdom from the Holy Spirit and know the true and pure

---

[2] "All Scripture is given by inspiration of God and is profitable for doctrine, for reproof, for correction, for instruction in righteousness: that the man of God may be perfect, thoroughly furnished unto all good works" (II Timothy 3:16-17).

gospel of Jesus Christ so well that when you hear a false gospel it may not easily deceive you.

One practical means the Lord has given for the protection of your faith is the local Bible-believing church. Here the means of grace are given: the Word (especially the preaching); prayer; and the sacraments (Baptism and the Lord's Supper). Do not neglect this solemn assembly of the people of God and membership therein. Among other purposes, God has given the church, His own body, for the protection of His people from the wolves seeking to devour with their clever fables.

37

False Teachers Part 4: Their Devices

Is there not still a prophet of the LORD here, that we may inquire of Him?" So the king of Israel said to Jehoshaphat, "There is still one man, Micaiah the son of Imlah, by whom we may inquire of the LORD; but I hate him, because he does not prophesy good concerning me, but evil." And Jehoshaphat said, "Let not the king say such things!" Then the king of Israel called an officer and said, "Bring Micaiah the son of Imlah quickly!"

The king of Israel and Jehoshaphat the king of Judah, having put on their robes, sat each on his throne, at a threshing floor at the entrance of the gate of Samaria; and all the prophets prophesied before them. Now Zedekiah the son of Chenaanah had made horns of iron for himself; and he said, "Thus says the LORD: 'With these you shall gore the Syrians until they are destroyed.' " And all the prophets prophesied so, saying, "Go up to Ramoth Gilead and prosper, for the LORD will deliver it into the king's hand."

I Kings 22:7-12 NKJV

Jesus warned us in Matthew 24:24 that false prophets would show great signs and wonders in their deceit. Their signs today are elaborate, dazzling, and expensive.

The performance at the gate of Samaria must have been something to behold. Two kings together with their armies, servants, and retinues, 400 prophets, one of whom, Zedekiah, came forward with a dramatic prophecy. He made for himself horns of iron that he either wore on his head or carried in his hands to demonstrate just how great the defeat of Syria would be.

As horns of a bull can gore a man to death, so Ahab would gore the king of Syria until he was destroyed.

The great victories against Syria were likely still on the minds of Ahab and these prophets. Twice by the Word of the Lord, Ahab had gone up and defeated Ben-Hadad. Now it was by Ahab's own word that he wished to go up a third time, and in dramatic fashion his prophets gave him signs to confirm his desire.

How great are the shows and messages of false prophets today who come from elaborate temples and churches. They come with pomp and expense, staff, support, lighting, drama to tell a message that often leaves the hearer still hungry for the truth as was Jehoshaphat, who by the grace of God saw right through these devices. Can we see through these devices?

How attractive are the shows and theatrics put on by so many? Some have shows of humility; consider the supposed impoverished life of Roman Catholic priests and nuns.[1] Some have shows of excess and prosperity; consider the televangelists flying around in jets and calling upon their followers to send money so they can buy bigger jets.

Paul tells us if any comes preaching another gospel than the gospel he has preached, which comes from the Lord Himself, the same gospel that Jesus preached, let him be accursed. Many phony gospels have come, are here, and will come. Do not fall for them. Hold fast only to the pure gospel of the Lord Jesus Christ

---

[1] In 1965 Time Magazine estimated the wealth of the Vatican at $10 - $15 billion. Today many sources agree that the wealth of the Roman Catholic Church is impossible to tell. The real estate owned by the church alone is likely worth tens of billions or hundreds of billions of dollars. And yet, around the world the church pleads for the poor to give more to build more wealth and outward show for the 'church.' The shepherds of Rome rob the houses of the poor, orphans, and widows to feed their own bellies. For a pretense they make themselves to care for the poor while they plunder those they vow to serve and extend almost nothing of their own resources in support.

who saves by His grace alone through faith alone in Christ alone who is found in the Scripture alone all for the Glory of God alone. There is no other name in heaven or in earth whereby men might be saved but the name of Jesus Christ. Listen to Him. Christ has the words of everlasting life. Where else can you possibly go? Go to Christ!

38

Speak Encouragement

Then the messenger who had gone to call Micaiah spoke to him, saying, Now listen, the words of the prophets with one accord encourage the king. Please, let your word be like the word of one of them, and speak encouragement.

I Kings 22:13 NKJV

What does encouragement mean to you? I am unable to count the many times I have heard Christians speaking of encouraging unbelievers.

Merriam-Webster's dictionary defines encouragement in a few ways including "to inspire with courage, spirit, or hope," and "to spur on."

In the English Bible the word "encourage" and its derivatives are rarely used. When this word is used it often refers to urging someone towards a specific action. "He sent the priests in their changes, and encouraged them to the service of the house of the LORD" (2 Chron 35:2). "They encourage themselves in an evil matter..." (Psalm 64:5).

There is a desire to give people hope outside of or apart from the only one that can give hope, Jesus Christ. But if we bring Jesus Christ to an unbeliever we risk offending him or her rather than inspiring them so sometimes we think we can encourage without telling the truth of one's estate apart from Christ and the hope of salvation in Christ.

This is precisely what the servant of Ahab wanted the real prophet of the Lord, Micaiah, to do when he met with Ahab and Jehoshaphat. Do what the other prophets did and "speak encouragement" to Ahab regarding his desire to go up to battle with Syria.

Christians should never be confused about where encouragement, hope, motivation, and courage come from. True encouragement can only come from the Word of the true God. There is nothing encouraging to the lost family of a dead unbeliever to tell them lies like "he is in a better place" or that they "will see him again."[1] One is a lie, the other is cruel assuming the family will go to hell as well, never hearing the gospel. True encouragement calls the unbelieving family of an unbelieving friend, to believe in Jesus Christ who wipes away all tears, will raise the dead, and brings the dead in Christ to be with Him in paradise forever.

True encouragement can only come from truth. Hearing flattery or lies may make people feel better for a bit but has no positive effect and may actually leave the lost sinner thinking falsely that he is at peace with God whom he has never been reconciled with through the blood of Christ.

As we step out into a dying world, the lost will desire encouragement from you and affirmation in their every evil way. Give them encouragement. But give them encouragement to repent of sin, believe in Christ, and lead a godly life, for to have Christ is to have the greatest encouragement of all.

---

[1] These kind and true words are only kind and true for Christians and their families and should be reserved for the same. The misuse of these truths with unbelievers has blunted the impact of their use with Christians. Let's reclaim the truth that for Christians "to live is Christ and to die is gain." Those who die in the Lord we shall see again in Heaven and at the great day of Resurrection (I Thessalonians 4). Praise be to the Lord!

39

Faithful Prophets: Micaiah the Son of Imlah

"And Micaiah said, " As the LORD lives, whatever the LORD says to me, that I will speak." Then he came to the king; and the king said to him, "Micaiah, shall we go to war against Ramoth Gilead, or shall we refrain?" And he answered him, "Go and prosper, for the LORD will deliver it into the hand of the king!" So the king said to him, "How many times shall I make you swear that you tell me nothing but the truth in the name of the LORD?" Then he said, "I saw all Israel scattered on the mountains, as sheep that have no shepherd. And the LORD said, 'These have no master. Let each return to his house in peace.' " And the king of Israel said to Jehoshaphat, "Did I not tell you he would not prophesy good concerning me, but evil?"

I Kings 22:14-18 NKJV

William Hunter at the young age of 19 was one of many Reformed Christians who was burned at the stake under Bloody Mary's reign[1] for holding to the Word of God over the word of the pope. After his imprisonment for refusing to take part in the mass, he was urged many times, even up to the moment of his execution to recant his faith and submit to Rome. He would, however, only do one thing; submit himself to the Word of God. Since the Word of God said Christ suffered and died once and for all for the remission of sins, he would believe the Word over the pope, who claimed Christ must continuously be

---

[1] Mary I of England (1516 - 1558) used much of her power and resources to put down through persecution the Protestant Reformation in England.

offered. With that simple, seemingly harmless confession, he was burned to death at the stake.

We know little of Micaiah the prophet, other than his father's name. We do not know which city he came from in Israel, his age, history, etc. The only account of him given in Scripture is this passage in I Kings 22 and the parallel account in II Chronicles 18. But while the Lord does not reveal to us the things we celebrate in people today, academic, athletic, financial, and professional achievements, the Lord does reveal to us that which is most important and for which we should all desire to be known: Micaiah was a faithful servant of the Lord.

Four hundred prophets told Ahab the flattering message he wanted to hear. Micaiah went to Ahab to tell him: "whatever the Lord says to me" (vs. 14). Here is the mark of a true prophet, preacher, and teacher of the Word: He tells the Word of God. Unintimidated by the messages of the numerous false prophets or the hatred of the pure Word of God, the faithful prophet receives the Word of God in the Scripture and tells it to all who will hear.

Micaiah was known to Ahab and Ahab to Micaiah. They had a history together. Ahab did not like him because Micaiah told him the truth when all Ahab really wanted was soothing lies. [2]With this history in mind and in accordance with Elijah at Mt. Carmel, Micaiah came with a godly mocking of the 400 prophets by echoing their message (vs. 13). Micaiah showed Ahab and Jehoshaphat how silly and transparent the message of the false prophets really was. Anyone can say what you want to hear. The

---

[2] How many have left the church and the Christian faith because they did not like the message they heard from the Word of God? Faithful preaching will make us uncomfortable at times and ought to if it is to reveal and convict us of our sin and unrighteousness. How can we become more like Christ if we know not where we are opposed to Christ? Do not run from faithful preaching because it pricks your conscious but, confess your sin to the Lord and humble yourself before the Almighty.

difficult message to hear and say is the truth. At Ahab's rebuke and urging, Micaiah then gave the vision from the Lord: "I saw all Israel scattered upon the hills, as sheep that have no shepherd..." (vs. 17).

We should learn several things from this passage:

First, the mercy of the Lord is very great to warn us of our sin and pending judgment. Ahab was warned many times by several prophets. Nineveh was warned in the end by Jonah alone and with a very limited sermon. If we hear the warning, heed it (repent), and have faith in Christ, we shall be saved from the judgment.

Second, the long-suffering of the Lord is very great. Ahab's judgment from our perspective was very long in coming. The wicked often live long lives, and sometimes the righteous are cut short in their days. This gives the wicked even more time for repentance while the righteous are forever with the Lord.

Third, the long-suffering of the Lord is not a forever-suffering of the Lord. The day of the Lord's judgment will come upon all men, for all have sinned. Ahab's judgment finally came. The Lord will not withhold his wrath forever so while it is still today "hear his voice, harden not your hearts as in the provocation... but exhort one another daily, while it is still called today; lest any of you be hardened through the deceitfulness of sin. For we are made partakers of Christ, if we hold the beginning of our confidence steadfast unto the end" (Hebrew 3:7-8, 13-14).

Finally, let us learn that against any intimidation, opposition, threat, or fear, like William Hunter and Micaiah the son of Imlah, we can stand confident and firm on the Word of God and the God of the Word, who endures forever!

40

The Terror of Unbelief

Then Micaiah said, "Therefore hear the word of the LORD: I saw the LORD sitting on His throne, and all the host of heaven standing by, on His right hand and on His left. And the LORD said, 'Who will persuade Ahab to go up, that he may fall at Ramoth Gilead?' So one spoke in this manner, and another spoke in that manner. Then a spirit came forward and stood before the LORD, and said, 'I will persuade him.' The LORD said to him, 'In what way?' So he said, 'I will go out and be a lying spirit in the mouth of all his prophets.' And the LORD said, 'You shall persuade him, and also prevail. Go out and do so.' Therefore look! The LORD has put a lying spirit in the mouth of all these prophets of yours, and the LORD has declared disaster against you."
I Kings 22:19-23 NKJV

Every so often in Scripture the Lord gives us a glimpse into His throne room in Heaven,[1] where we read of sights too amazing for our finite, mortal minds to comprehend. In verse 19, Micaiah was taken in a vision to the throne room of the Lord where "all the host of heaven [was] standing by, on His right hand and on His left." What does "all the host of heaven" include? The angels? What about the fallen angels? Are the righteous on the right and the fallen on the left? Is this the same place and gathering where Satan met with the Lord and discussed Job (Job 1:6-12)? Many questions arise that the Lord has not answered for us, and we must rest content that these secret things belong to Him. However, in the middle of these mysterious visions, the Lord still revealed a conversation for us to understand.

As the host was gathered by the Lord's throne in Heaven, the Lord asked who would persuade Ahab to go to battle in Ramoth Gilead

---

[1] Isaiah 6:1, Ezekiel 1:26; Daniel 7:9; Revelation (Especially chapters 3-7)

so that he might be killed there. The Lord had purposed for Ahab to die in battle so it would certainly come to pass. Then "a spirit came forward... and said, "I will persuade him... I will go out and be a lying spirit in the mouth of all his prophets" (vs. 22). The Lord confirmed this would be successful and allowed the lying spirit to proceed to the 400 prophets of Ahab (vs. 22).

Have you ever considered that you may be a topic of conversation for the Lord with His heavenly host? This was the case for Job (a righteous man) and Ahab (an unrighteousness man). We may think because the Lord does not speak to us from the clouds today that He does not care so much about us and that our actions have little bearing on the future. The opposite is true. He who sees and knows all carries out His perfect purposes.

Ahab used Micaiah's prophecy as proof to Jehoshaphat that Micaiah simply had it in for him. Ahab's argument was that Micaiah could not be telling the truth because every word Micaiah spoke about him was bad. In order to prove the prophecy was true, Micaiah revealed greater background to his prophecy through the conversation in heaven.

Micaiah's vision was one final warning to wicked Ahab: "Look, the Lord has put a lying spirit in the mouth of all these prophets of yours, and the Lord has declared disaster against you" (vs. 23).

In this last phase of Ahab's terrible life, the Lord revealed a terrifying message to Ahab. Ahab should have been running from the wrath of God, falling down on his face, pleading with God for mercy at this late hour of desperate need. If Ramoth Gilead was north, Ahab should have gotten into his chariot and headed south. Instead, Ahab hardened his heart and would not listen.

Telling the truth (sharing the Word) to our families and friends includes at times giving difficult messages. Not all who hear our report of the grace of God in Christ will believe it. To some, the gospel will minister greater judgment, for it will leave those like

Ahab who don't believe in greater sin. To others, however, the gospel will minister salvation and eternal life through Jesus Christ. May the Lord use this passage to humble the Christian before the Almighty and give the fear of the Lord that is the beginning of wisdom to the unbeliever that he might be saved.

41

The Mark of a True Prophet

Now Zedekiah the son of Chenaanah went near and struck Micaiah on the cheek, and said, "Which way did the spirit from the LORD go from me to speak to you?" And Micaiah said, "Indeed, you shall see on that day when you go into an inner chamber to hide!" So the king of Israel said, "Take Micaiah, and return him to Amon the governor of the city and to Joash the king's son; and say, "Thus says the king: Put this fellow in prison, and feed him with bread of affliction and water of affliction, until I come in peace." 'But Micaiah said, "If you ever return in peace, the LORD has not spoken by me." And he said, "Take heed, all you people!"

I Kings 22:24-28 NKJV

When Jesus was being examined by the High Priest and the Sanhedrin in Matthew 26 they spat on His face, beat Him, struck Him, and then mocked Him by saying, "Prophecy! Who is the one who struck You?"

Do you remember Zedekiah who put on the show for Ahab and Jehoshaphat with the bull horns (v.11)? That same Zedekiah was still around for Micaiah's prophecy and responded by striking Micaiah on the cheek and mocked him as Micaiah's Savior would be mocked and beaten in years to come.

Jesus calmly told the High Priest he would see the Son of Man on the throne of power. Micaiah told Zedekiah, he would see about the lying spirit on the day he would hide in his home for fear of his life. The wicked may look like they are winning for a moment, but the end is already written. They will be destroyed. The righteous have nothing to fear when God is on His throne, ruling and reigning and bringing all His enemies under His footstool.

For his prophecy, Micaiah was taken and thrown into prison with, at best, terrible tasting-bread and water. He was to be there until Ahab returned because of his unhelpful prophecy. In front of all the gathering, Micaiah boldly declared that if Ahab returned from Ramoth Gilead then Micaiah was not a true prophet of the Lord. But if Ahab did not return, then all the people should take note that Micaiah had previously told of this from the mouth of the Lord Himself.

Micaiah reminded the people of the Word of the Lord in the days of Moses.[1] If Ahab returned in peace, Micaiah was not from God because his prophecy did not come to pass. But, the opposite was also true. If Ahab did not return from Ramoth Gilead alive then Micaiah was a prophet of the Lord. Let the people judge.

Why should we trust the promises (prophecies) of the Lord concerning those things which we have not seen because they have not yet come to pass? Why should we believe that the resurrection at the last day and the life everlasting is true? I have seen many die but I have never seen any come back to life. Why should I believe God's promises for the future?

Because all that the Lord has promised concerning past events in history has come to pass. All that the Lord has purposed, He has also done. Consider God's promise to Abraham, Isaac, and Jacob that He would bring them to the Promised Land - even after bondage in Egypt. He did as He promised. Consider the prophecy of Isaiah, "the virgin shall conceive and bear a Son..." and Mary gave birth to Jesus. Consider Jesus who said, "I have power to lay

---

[1] "But the prophet who presumes to speak a word in My name, which I have not commanded him to speak, or who speaks in the name of other gods, that prophet shall die... when a prophet speaks in the name of the LORD, if the thing does not happen or come to pass, that is the thing which the LORD has not spoken" (Deut. 18:20-22).

down My life and to raise it up again..." and did. Consider Ahab who was told he would die in Ramoth Gilead. Lord willing in our next study we will see that to be true as well.

The Lord is faithful in all His ways, true in all His promises. You can rest assured in the promises of the Lord for the future because your God has been faithful and true in all of His promises in the past. All that He has said He would do, He has done, is doing, and will do. On that great day of the Lord you will see with your eyes what you now see by faith. May all the world take heed!

42

Ahab's Demise

"So the king of Israel and Jehoshaphat the king of Judah went up to Ramoth Gilead. And the king of Israel said to Jehoshaphat, "I will disguise myself and go into battle; but you put on your robes." So the king of Israel disguised himself and went into battle. Now the king of Syria had commanded the thirty-two captains of his chariots, saying, "Fight with no one small or great, but only with the king of Israel." So it was, when the captains of the chariots saw Jehoshaphat, that they said, "Surely it is the king of Israel!" Therefore they turned aside to fight against him, and Jehoshaphat cried out. And it happened, when the captains of the chariots saw that it was not the king of Israel, that they turned back from pursuing him.

Now a certain man drew a bow at random, and struck the king of Israel between the joints of his armor. So he said to the driver of his chariot, "Turn around and take me out of the battle, for I am wounded." The battle increased that day; and the king was propped up in his chariot, facing the Syrians, and died at evening. The blood ran out from the wound onto the floor of the chariot. Then, as the sun was going down, a shout went throughout the army, saying, "Every man to his city, and every man to his own country!" So the king died, and was brought to Samaria. And they buried the king in Samaria. Then someone washed the chariot at a pool in Samaria, and the dogs licked up his blood while the harlots bathed, according to the word of the LORD which He had spoken.

Now the rest of the acts of Ahab, and all that he did, the ivory house which he built and all the cities that he built, are they not written in the book of the chronicles of the kings of Israel? So Ahab rested with his fathers. Then Ahaziah his son reigned in his place.

I Kings 22:29-40 NKJV

When I was a child my siblings and I listened to Judy Rogers's songs from time to time on cassette tape and now we have some of her music downloaded into our car. One of her children's catechism songs begins like this, simple lyrics expressing a divine truth:

I'm hiding from mommy and no one can see
I'm hiding and no one will know!
But I just remembered that God's watching me;
He knows everything that I do.

We cannot hide from the omniscient, all-seeing God. In the final act of Ahab's life, he thought he could thwart any plan of the Lord by disguising himself as an ordinary soldier instead of going into battle dressed as a king. But the Lord was not fooled by clothing or position in the army. If the Syrian captains with one mission on the battlefield (vs. 31) could not find Ahab, a lone Syrian archer shooting without a target in mind certainly could. God's purposes surely stand.

All the ways men might pursue to avoid God's righteous judgment will be thwarted. Hiding from God will simply not work. Ahab's death was miserable. He was wounded without a great fight. He died even while his own army was being routed. His army was scattered like sheep without a shepherd, just as the prophet Micaiah had said (vs. 17). When his body was brought back to Samaria the dogs licked up his blood even while harlots bathed nearby (vs. 38). He who had led Israel into sin and sold himself to do evil died with dishonor. All that the Lord had spoken, He brought to pass.

We will not take a separate devotional on Jehoshaphat's 'salvation' but it must be noted. Thirty-two captains of Syria focused their attention on Jehoshaphat alone in the battle thinking him to be Ahab. In vs. 32, Jehoshaphat cried out and the captains recognized he was not their target and stopped pursuing him. In the parallel text in II Chronicles 18:31, "but Jehoshaphat cried out, and the Lord helped him, and God diverted them from him."

Jehoshaphat acted foolishly and sinfully in his alliance with Ahab against Syria. And yet, in his hour of need, the sense of the Scripture is that Jehoshaphat cried out to the Lord, who heard the cry of His servant and delivered him from the hands of the Syrians. The Lord did not owe this great kindness to Jehoshaphat. The Lord would have been just in allowing him to die in battle. But the Lord demonstrated His merciful kindness to His people yet again in delivering Jehoshaphat. We too can and should cry out to the Lord in the hour of our need, and He will deliver us even if that means bringing us to everlasting glory in Heaven through death itself.

Micaiah was thrown into prison for his prophecy to Ahab. He suffered beating, mocking, and bread of affliction. Yet the Lord used him to show all Israel gathered that day preparing for battle that the Lord is God. Perhaps not with the drama of Mt. Carmel, but nevertheless with great power, the Lord vindicated His name yet again to Israel and Judah and teaches us that salvation comes not with might, power, or cunning, but from the Lord who knows everything we do.

No king is saved by the multitude of an army; A mighty man is not delivered by great strength. A horse is a vain hope for safety; Neither shall it deliver any by its great strength. Behold, the eye of the LORD is on those who fear Him, On those who hope in His mercy, To deliver their soul from death, And to keep them alive in famine. Our soul waits for the LORD; He is our help and our shield. For our heart shall rejoice in Him, Because we have trusted in His holy name. Let Your mercy, O LORD, be upon us, Just as we hope in You.

Psalms 33:16-22 NKJV

43

Memorials of Sin: Jehoram & Ahaziah

Jehoshaphat the son of Asa had become king over Judah in the fourth year of Ahab king of Israel. Jehoshaphat was thirty-five years old when he became king, and he reigned twenty-five years in Jerusalem. His mother's name was Azubah the daughter of Shilhi. And he walked in all the ways of his father Asa. He did not turn aside from them, doing what was right in the eyes of the LORD. Nevertheless the high places were not taken away, for the people offered sacrifices and burned incense on the high places. Also Jehoshaphat made peace with the king of Israel. Now the rest of the acts of Jehoshaphat, the might that he showed, and how he made war, are they not written in the book of the chronicles of the kings of Judah? And the rest of the perverted persons, who remained in the days of his father Asa, he banished from the land.

There was then no king in Edom, only a deputy of the king. Jehoshaphat made merchant ships to go to Ophir for gold; but they never sailed, for the ships were wrecked at Ezion Geber. Then Ahaziah the son of Ahab said to Jehoshaphat, "Let my servants go with your servants in the ships." But Jehoshaphat would not. And Jehoshaphat rested with his fathers, and was buried with his fathers in the City of David his father. Then Jehoram his son reigned in his place.

Ahaziah the son of Ahab became king over Israel in Samaria in the seventeenth year of Jehoshaphat king of Judah, and reigned two years over Israel. He did evil in the sight of the LORD, and walked in the way of his father and in the way of his mother and in the way of Jeroboam the son of Nebat, who had made Israel sin; for he served Baal and worshiped him, and provoked the LORD God of Israel to anger, according to all that his father had done.

I Kings 22:41-53 NKJV

t is natural for children to learn from their parents' teaching. The Lord says, "Train up a child in the way he will go and when he is old he will not depart from it" (Prov. 22:6). The opposite also holds true: Train up a child in the wrong way to go, and when he is old he will not depart from it. II Kings comes to a close in a less than hopeful manner for Judah and Israel. We are introduced to two sons of two kings who become kings themselves on the occasion of their fathers' deaths: Jehoram, son of Jehoshaphat,[1] and Ahaziah, son of Ahab.

Jehoram learned only the sinful ways of his father-in-law[2] and not the faith of his father Jehoshaphat. He caused all of Judah to sin with him to the extent that Elijah the prophet wrote to him telling him that he would die of a terrible sickness because he did not walk "in the ways of Jehoshaphat [his] father" (II Chron. 21:12).

Ahaziah followed his father Ahab in the worship of many gods and rejection of the true God of Israel, Jehovah. Neither king took their respective warnings from the Lord through the mouth of Elijah as an opportunity to call upon the Lord in repentance, but rather each went to their grave in unbelief. When Jehoram died, Scripture tells us, no one sorrowed for him in Jerusalem (II Chron 21:19-20).

Fathers have a tremendous responsibility to their families. They are to love their wives as Christ loved the church. They are to teach their children the works of the Lord and instruct them in the most precious faith once for all delivered to the saints. They are to be examples for good to their children rather than evil. If I have

---

[1] Jehoram can be confusing in Kings and Chronicles because both Ahab and Jehoshaphat had sons named Jehoram (sometimes translated "Jorah") who became king. They also overlapped as kings for some time adding to the confusion. The shared names may have been due to the ungodly alliance between the two kings.

[2] Jehoram was married to the daughter of Ahab (II Chronicles 21:6)

learned anything in nearly ten years as a father it is that these things are much easier said than done. My best examples contain sin and the worst examples are only sin. What then can fallen fathers do as they seek to teach their children?

Confess your sins before the Lord and your children; delight yourself in the Word of the Lord; trust in Christ with all your heart, soul, strength, and mind; and pray without ceasing. Children figure out pretty quickly that their parents are not perfect. However, if parents pretend to be perfect and never acknowledge their own sin, children are well on the way to rebellion and rejection of their parents' faith. Fathers and mothers must not be stubborn and proud before those who know them best but must repent to the Lord and acknowledge and apologize for the sins against their children or public sins against the Lord. Scripture does not tell us if Jehoshaphat ever confessed his sins of unholy alliances with Israel. Clearly, Jehoram learned to love the ways of those with whom Jehoshaphat aligned himself.

The devil and his followers will certainly come after our children tempting them to reject the faith for many reasons, including the clear sins of their parents. What greater defeat of this snare than when our children can answer the doubts of the evil one with, "Yes, it is true, my father and my mother are sinners too who confess their sins before the Lord, acknowledge them before the world, and trust in the Lord Jesus Christ of grace and mercy for the forgiveness of their sins and eternal life." Let us not present to our children a false faith hoping in time to come they will discover the truth but rather let us reveal the true Christian faith and the life of repentance we are called to live.

A note for wives and mothers: The focus of this devotional is on fathers as it is the focus of this portion of II Kings. Nevertheless, many of these lessons have direct overlap with mothers and wives. If you go further into the larger context of these two kings you will see the impact of wives and mothers for evil (Jezebel and Athaliah in particular) as well as for good (Azubah and others). May all men and women live lives of devotion to the Lord.

44

Looking for Help in All the Wrong Places

*Moab rebelled against Israel after the death of Ahab. Now
Ahaziah fell through the lattice of his upper room in Samaria, and
was injured; so he sent messengers and said to them, Go, inquire
of Baal-Zebub, the god of Ekron, whether I shall recover from this
injury.*

*But the angel of the LORD said to Elijah the Tishbite, Arise, go up
to meet the messengers of the king of Samaria, and say to them,
Is it because there is no God in Israel that you are going to inquire
of Baal-Zebub, the god of Ekron? Now therefore, thus says the
LORD: You shall not come down from the bed to which you have
gone up, but you shall surely die.*

*So Elijah departed. And when the messengers returned to him, he
said to them, Why have you come back? So they said to him, "A
man came up to meet us, and said to us, Go, return to the king
who sent you, and say to him, Thus says the LORD: Is it because
there is no God in Israel that you are sending to inquire of Baal-
Zebub, the god of Ekron? Therefore you shall not come down from
the bed to which you have gone up, but you shall surely die. Then
he said to them, What kind of man was it who came up to meet
you and told you these words? So they answered him, A hairy man
wearing a leather belt around his waist. And he said, It is Elijah the
Tishbite.*

II Kings 1:1-8 NKJV

I have not read the book "Lord of the flies" but I do know its title
was not original. The original Lord of the Flies was one of the
idols of the Philistine city of Ekron and the same false god

Ahaziah desired to consult after he was injured falling through a door or window in an upper room. The name in Scripture is Baal-Zebub, literally translated, "Lord of the Flies."

Ahaziah witnessed much in his youth. He saw all the wickedness of his parents, Ahab and Jezebel. He saw the mockery the Lord made of them through Elijah and the other prophets. He saw Baal unable to answer the 450 prophets on Mt. Carmel. After he ascended the throne of his father, he served and worshipped Baal who let down his father before him (I Kings 22:53). It is often the case that children grow up to fall into the same sins of their parents before him.

The Lord of truth, Jehovah, had proved Himself to be the only God of truth all of the days of Ahaziah and yet in his hour of need, Ahaziah looked to the god of the Philistines for help.

Ahaziah's messengers were en route to Ekron when the messenger of the Lord called Elijah to intercept them (vs. 3). Elijah challenged the messengers as to the reason for their journey. Was it because there was no God in Israel that they went to inquire of the Lord of the Flies, the god of Ekron? Clearly there is a God in Israel, only His people have rejected Him.

Elijah gave a prophecy to the messengers from the Lord to Ahaziah: You will not get better from your injuries but will surely die. The messengers delivered the message to Ahaziah. A similar message was given to King Hezekiah many years later in Isaiah 37:2. He took the news and cried unto the Lord for mercy, which the Lord showed to him and he was healed. Ahaziah did no such thing. Instead he wanted to know who the prophet was since Ahaziah had previous encounters with messengers of the Lord. The king's messengers reported the man was hairy and wearing a leather belt. That was enough for Ahaziah to know it was Elijah the Tishbite.

What darkness of the soul seeks for help in the hour of need from a dumb god who cannot speak, walk, see, hear, or act? Where will you seek for help in your hour of need? The world seeks for it in all the wrong places, but there is one place where help can be found. The psalmist says, "My help comes from the LORD, Who made heaven and earth" (Psalm 121:2). This is the constant message of the prophets: The Lord, He is God. Turn to the Lord Jesus Christ today and find help in Him for all sickness, disease, and distress.

Postscript: In the Greek, this Baal-Zebub is changed to "Beelzebub" a name for Satan himself (Matthew 10:25; 12:24, 27; Mark 3:22; Luke 11:15,18,19). It has the same meaning as the Hebrew name but with a focus more in the Greek on the prince of flies or perhaps more appropriately, 'prince of the demonic flies.' Strong's Exhaustive Concordance translates Beelzebub as 'dung-god,' highlighting the folly of following idolatry. It is no different from worshipping dung as your god.

45

Thou Shalt Not Take the Name of the Lord Thy God in Vain

Then the king sent to him a captain of fifty with his fifty men. So he went up to him; and there he was, sitting on the top of a hill. And he spoke to him: Man of God, the king has said, Come down! So Elijah answered and said to the captain of fifty, If I am a man of God, then let fire come down from heaven and consume you and your fifty men. And fire came down from heaven and consumed him and his fifty. Then he sent to him another captain of fifty with his fifty men. And he answered and said to him: Man of God, thus has the king said, Come down quickly! So Elijah answered and said to them, If I am a man of God, let fire come down from heaven and consume you and your fifty men. And the fire of God came down from heaven and consumed him and his fifty.

II Kings 1:9-12 NKJV

The Westminster Shorter Catechism Question number 55 asks "What is forbidden in the third commandment?" The answer is: "The third commandment forbiddeth all profaning or abusing of anything whereby God maketh himself known." A very straight-forward answer. For this reason, the Ark of the Covenant was not to be touched except by the Levites. It was not be opened except perhaps by the High Priest on a special occasion. The Lord's Supper is not to be taken lightly lest it be profaned. In these two elements of worship (an Old and New Testament element) God made/makes Himself known.

In The Old Testament, in addition to the Ark and other objects and places, the Lord also made Himself known through His prophets. The prophet of the Lord spoke the Word of the Lord and was a representative of the Lord. To malign or abuse the prophet of the Lord was in many contexts the same as profaning God's name. Korah's rebellion against Moses was in reality against God who established Moses.

When King Ahaziah sent his captains to do that which Jezebel's captains could not accomplish - capture or kill Elijah - the first two captains came to Elijah mocking his title. "Man of God, the king has said, Come down!" (vs. 9). "Man of God, thus has the king said, Come down quickly!" (Vs. 11).

The way these men spoke to Elijah was evil for several reasons: 1) As Keil and Delitzsch explain, it showed contempt for the prophetic office Elijah held as the spokesman of the Lord; 2) It showed contempt for the Lord Himself who sent Elijah as His servant; and 3) The captains' contempt for the prophet elevated the authority of the word of the king above the Word of God.

Elijah answered their mockery with their own words. "If I am a man of God, then let fire come down from heaven and consume you and your fifty men." This fire the Lord sent twice, consuming the two captains and their fifty men just as He consumed the sacrifice on Mt. Carmel with fire some years before, "...for the Lord will not hold him guiltless who takes His name in vain" (Exodus 20:7).

May the Lord use this portion of His Word to teach us to "reverence His names, titles, attributes, ordinances, Word, and works."

46

Walk Humbly With Your God

Again, he sent a third captain of fifty with his fifty men. And the third captain of fifty went up, and came and fell on his knees before Elijah, and pleaded with him, and said to him: Man of God, please let my life and the life of these fifty servants of yours be precious in your sight. Look, fire has come down from heaven and burned up the first two captains of fifties with their fifties. But let my life now be precious in your sight.

And the angel of the LORD said to Elijah, Go down with him; do not be afraid of him. So he arose and went down with him to the king. Then he said to him, Thus says the LORD: Because you have sent messengers to inquire of Baal-Zebub, the god of Ekron, is it because there is no God in Israel to inquire of His word? Therefore you shall not come down from the bed to which you have gone up, but you shall surely die.

So Ahaziah died according to the word of the LORD which Elijah had spoken. Because he had no son, Jehoram became king in his place, in the second year of Jehoram the son of Jehoshaphat, king of Judah. Now the rest of the acts of Ahaziah which he did, are they not written in the book of the chronicles of the kings of Israel?

II Kings 1:13-18 NKJV

Some might call the recent portions of Kings depressing for the constant sin on display. Certainly these chapters present many examples for us to learn from. See how these kings, prophets, and captains rebelled? Do not follow in their footsteps. But something else happens when reading lengthy portions of Scripture dealing with sin. When a humble man appears on the scene as the third captain in verse 13 and 14, it is like an ice cold lemonade from Chick-fil-A on a sweltering hot day after many hours of outdoor physical labor.

The third captain stands apart from his fellow captains who were reduced to ash along with their commands. He was a servant of King Ahaziah and obeyed him as far as he was able to obey the Lord. But this third captain would not speak sinfully to Elijah. Instead he came humbly before him, falling on his knees, and pleaded with Elijah as a man of God to spare his life and the life of his soldiers.

The Lord did not forget the cry of the humble captain[1] but delivered him and his soldiers from the fire from heaven that consumed the previous 102 men. The angel of the Lord advised Elijah to go with the soldiers, they went, and Elijah repeated his prophecy directly to Ahaziah. Because Ahaziah inquired of Baal-Zebub, the god of Ekron, and we might add, because he never repented of this wickedness, Ahaziah would never rise from his bed again but would die. And he did.

How easy is it to be puffed up with pride and arrogance? We are warned that pride goes before destruction (Prov. 16:18) and that a man's pride shall bring him low, but honor shall uphold the humble in spirit (Prov. 29:23).

The Lord has called us to a life of humility, for this was the life of Christ on earth. "Let this mind be in you which was also in Christ Jesus, who, being in the form of God, did not consider it robbery to be equal with God, but made Himself of no reputation, taking the form of a bond servant, and coming in the likeness of men. And being found in appearance as man, He humbled Himself and became obedient to the point of death, even the death of the cross" (Phil. 2:5-8).

---

[1] Psalm 9:2b: "He does not forget the cry of the humble." Psalm 10:17: "LORD, You have heard the desire of the humble; You will prepare their heart; You will cause Your ear to hear..."

Through the work of the Lord in humbling this captain's heart, he retained honor in the eyes of generations to come. Will you be a man or woman of humility, even submitting yourself to the righteous law of God? If we are hasty, let us be hasty in obedience to the Lord. If we are slow, may we be slow to accuse. If we are given to boasting, may we boast only in the cross of Christ who is our all in all. If we walk, may we walk humbly before the Lord today.

47

Elijah's Ascension Part 1:
The Comfort of the Lord

And it came to pass, when the LORD was about to take up Elijah into heaven by a whirlwind, that Elijah went with Elisha from Gilgal. Then Elijah said to Elisha, "Stay here, please, for the LORD has sent me on to Bethel." But Elisha said, " As the LORD lives, and as your soul lives, I will not leave you!" So they went down to Bethel. Now the sons of the prophets who were at Bethel came out to Elisha, and said to him, "Do you know that the LORD will take away your master from over you today?" And he said, "Yes, I know; keep silent!" Then Elijah said to him, "Elisha, stay here, please, for the LORD has sent me on to Jericho." But he said, " As the LORD lives, and as your soul lives, I will not leave you!" So they came to Jericho. Now the sons of the prophets who were at Jericho came to Elisha and said to him, "Do you know that the LORD will take away your master from over you today?" So he answered, "Yes, I know; keep silent!" Then Elijah said to him, "Stay here, please, for the LORD has sent me on to the Jordan." But he said, " As the LORD lives, and as your soul lives, I will not leave you!" So the two of them went on.

II Kings 2:1-6 NKJV

If you knew that your time on earth was drawing towards a close, how would you spend your final days? The Lord Jesus Christ spent His final days on earth instructing, teaching, exhorting, encouraging, and comforting the church. He revealed His resurrected body to hundreds of people including many times to His disciples. He promised the Holy Spirit (John 14 and 16; Acts 1:5-8) of comfort and reminded them that He had all power in heaven and in earth.

As I have visited with elderly saints close to death, they have been a great comfort and encouragement to me in the faith. As they drew closer to glory, I went to minister to them and left having been ministered to by them.

Elijah, an Old Testament type of Christ,[1] foreshadowed the manner in which Christ Himself entered heaven by ascending from earth to heaven in the flesh when he had finished the work he was called to do. But before this miracle took place in the sight of many witnesses, Elijah was called to one more task: to visit the sons of the prophets (vs. 3 and 5).

We should observe that: 1) The Lord had prepared Elijah and Israel for this time of Elijah's exit from earth; 2) The Lord was answering the cry of His servant back in the wilderness (I Kings 18:4); 3) The Lord had revealed the upcoming event to Elisha and the sons of the prophets; and 4) The Lord had called, anointed, and prepared Elisha to take up the work from Elijah.

The time had come for Elijah's work to be completed. The final task of the Lord was for Elijah to make a triangular route from Gilgal to Bethel, to Jericho, and finally across the Jordan River where he would be taken up in a whirlwind.

On his way he visited the sons of the prophets in Bethel and Jericho. Here were cities of sin (Jeroboam had constructed a golden calf for worship in Bethel (I Kings 12: 28-29) and Jericho was rebuilt against the word of the Lord) where the truth of God's Word was still being spread by faithful prophets. Elijah was a friend to these prophets. He had been like a father to them and to

---

[1] Jesus Christ ascended up into heaven of His own power, for He is fully God and fully man, in two distinct natures, and one person, forever. Neither Elijah nor any other prophet could perform miracles or ascend up into heaven of his own power, for they were not God but were mere men. For this reason and others, Elijah and other Old Testament figures are called "types" of Christ, as they are not Christ but point people to Jesus Christ and the work that He would do.

Israel, warning it of its sin, calling it to repent, and soon he would be no longer with them.

As the Lord comforted His disciples with the promise of the Holy Spirit before His ascension, so the visit of Elijah comforted the prophets and encouraged them in their work before he ascended into Heaven. It also had the providential effect of revealing to them Elisha's closeness to Elijah and the pending transfer of the mantle.

Those we love much will leave us for a time, and one day we will leave others we love much. May we not forget to comfort those we love so as to strengthen them in their faith. The Lord Jesus Christ never leaves us or forsakes us, but is with us always, even to the end of the age. He has given us the gift of the Spirit to continue to comfort us until we see Him face to face.

48

Elijah's Ascension, Part 2:
The Preparation of the Lord

And fifty men of the sons of the prophets went and stood facing them at a distance, while the two of them stood by the Jordan. Now Elijah took his mantle, rolled it up, and struck the water; and it was divided this way and that, so that the two of them crossed over on dry ground. And so it was, when they had crossed over, that Elijah said to Elisha, "Ask! What may I do for you, before I am taken away from you?" Elisha said, "Please let a double portion of your spirit be upon me." So he said, "You have asked a hard thing. Nevertheless, if you see me when I am taken from you, it shall be so for you; but if not, it shall not be so.

II Kings 2:7-10 NKJV

There are some people that pass from this life to the next without whom we do not think we can live or carry on our work. As children, we may think this way about our parents. As adults, we may think this way about our children or spouse. As Christians, we may think this way about a pastor or theologian who has helped us come to know Christ more fully. For the believers in Israel, the person they did not want to live without was the great prophet Elijah. When Elijah was carried up to Heaven in verse 11, Elisha called him, "My father, my father, the chariot of Israel and its horsemen."

Nevertheless, the Lord does not leave His people when they experience great change or loss in their lives. He who is the Almighty God is also the kind Father, and He prepares us for those great and terrible days when those we love dearly and hold in high esteem depart from this life to the life to come. He prepares us in at least three ways: 1) by His Word; 2) by His works; and 3) by His Spirit.

As Elijah went from place to place he asked Elisha to stay and allow him to depart alone. In each instance Elisha refused to leave Elijah so long as the Lord lived and Elijah's soul lived. Since we have souls that can never die and the Lord God always was, always is, and always will be, Elisha was saying, "I will not leave you until the Lord takes you away from me." As he went the sons of the prophets confirmed God's Word to Elisha: "Do you know that the Lord will take away your master from over you today: (vs. 3 and 5). As Elisha prepared to lose his closest friend on earth and father in the faith, the Word of the Lord through the prophets prepared Elisha for that great and terrible hour.

Until the Jordan River, God had been preparing Elisha through the testimony of His Word by the mouth of the prophets; but when they arrived at the Jordan River the Lord used another testimony for the comfort of Elisha: Elijah performed a miracle by the power of the Lord. Elijah struck the Jordan River with his mantle, and as the Lord drew apart the Jordan to create a gateway for the Israelites into Canaan so the Lord parted the Jordan this second time, preparing Elisha through this mighty work of the Lord and creating a gateway for Elijah's triumphal entry into the eternal promised land.

When they crossed over the Jordan on dry land, Elijah knew the time of his departure was near and did not try to dissuade Elisha from following but asked him what he could do for him. Elisha's request was wise: "Please let a double portion of your spirit be upon me" (vs. 9). This request has been translated in different ways, but I take it to mean Elisha was asking for even more (double) the Spirit of the Lord that had been with Elijah to be upon Elisha in his work that lay ahead. This was a hard request for Elijah, for it was not in his power to grant it. Who can give the Spirit of the Lord but the Lord Himself? Nevertheless, the Lord let Elisha know how this request would be answered. If Elisha saw

Elijah depart then the Lord had granted the request. If he did not see him depart then it was not granted.

The Lord prepared Elisha for the departure of his dearest friend with His Word, His Works, and His Spirit. He prepares us and carries us in this life in the same way. His Word, Works, and Spirit are all given to us for at least two reasons: 1) to comfort us through every trial, sorrow, and grief; and 2) to lead us on our Christian walk through whatever work the Lord has prepared for us, until at last we shall be conducted up into heaven and be with the Lord and His saints for all eternity. If you are reading this, that latter time has not yet come, but the former time is here. Let us go forth in service to the King.

49

Elijah's Ascension, Part 3:
The Method of the Lord

*Then it happened, as they continued on and talked, that suddenly
a chariot of fire appeared with horses of fire, and separated the
two of them; and Elijah went up by a whirlwind into heaven.*

II Kings 2:11 NKJV

The grace, mercy, and glory of the Lord is beyond all our comprehension. If we started listing the good deeds of the Lord we would never come to an end. The goodness of the Lord is infinite. The works of the Lord are exceedingly abundantly more than we could ask or think. The promises of God in Christ Jesus our Lord are true and secure. If our finite minds were to express the high point or culmination of all God's gifts to us, we might say with I John 2:25, "And this is the promise that He has promised us - eternal life."

The fathers of the faith all looked forward to eternal life. They knew with Paul that to live was Christ but to die was gain, for they looked for the city which has foundations whose Builder and Maker is God. All believers who have passed from this life to the next on account of the grace of God and the righteousness of Christ Jesus imputed to them are now enjoying the pleasures and sinlessness of that city where dwells the Lamb of God. But almost all share one common trait: They went down into the Valley of the Shadow of Death before they ascended to the City of the Lord forever. Two men did not share that process - Enoch and Elijah skipped the Valley and went straight to glory.[1]

---

[1] I borrowed this picture of skipping the Valley of the Shadow of Death from Matthew Henry who in turn credits a Mr. Crowley.

Elijah, zealous for the glory of the Lord, desired the Lord to allow him to die, yet the Lord honored His servant not by giving him death but by carrying him, body and soul, from earth on a chariot of fire drawn by horses of fire.

The chariot and horses of fire were angels of the Lord. We will see this later with Elisha at Dothan, and remember the words of Psalm 68:17: "The chariots of God are twenty thousand, even thousands of angels: the Lord is among them..."

Elijah did not prepare himself for entry into glory by meditating on Mt. Carmel or hiding in a cave on Mt. Horeb, or contemplating by a stream in the wilderness. He prepared himself by ministering to Elisha (vs. 11). What wonderful words of encouragement the younger prophet must have received in those minutes before Elijah's ascension into glory.[2]

One day we too will be carried up by the ministering spirits of God, the angels, to the New Jerusalem, the city of God. Elijah was carried up swiftly into glory, riding on a chariot, pulled by horses of fire, and brought up in a whirlwind. Our entrance into heaven will be swift. Our eyes will close on earth and in the twinkling of an eye, will open in heaven. What would the Lord have us to do until that time? As Elijah was going about the work of a prophet and ministering to Elisha, so may we go about the work God has called us to do for His glory, looking forward to that great and terrible day of our departure from this life to the life to come.

---

[2] This account should bring to our memory the end of Mark 16 and the beginning of Acts 1, which recounts Christ's ascension into heaven. Before His ascension into glory and the throne at the right hand of the Father, Jesus Christ spoke to His disciples. In the minutes before He ascended, Jesus gave His disciples the Great Commission and told them to stay in Jerusalem to await the Spirit of comfort and power that He had promised. Then Jesus was taken up in their sight into Heaven.

50

Elijah's Ascension, Part 4:
Concerning Glorification and an Intermediate State in the Old Testament

Then it happened, as they continued on and talked, that suddenly a chariot of fire appeared with horses of fire, and separated the two of them; and Elijah went up by a whirlwind into heaven.

II Kings 2:11 NKJV

We must not move on from Elijah's wonderful entrance into glory without examining three lessons, doctrines, and divine comforts our Lord Jesus Christ is teaching us by His Spirit and His Word. The first two we will consider today and the third tomorrow.

First, Elijah's entrance into glory with his body and soul together pictures for us the final resurrection and glory that awaits all believers. When we pray, "Thy kingdom come," we are praying for several things including that the "kingdom of glory might be hastened" (WSC #102). That kingdom of glory is the New Heavens and the New Earth where believers shall in body and in soul be with the Lord Jesus Christ for all eternity (I Thessalonians 4: 13-18). The Heaven we go to at death is primarily a place for the souls of believers, but it is not without the promise of the body and soul reunited for eternity. Enoch and Elijah are there in the flesh along with the King of Kings who sits enthroned in the flesh, Jesus Christ, who ascended up into Heaven after His resurrection and will soon descend with power and glory. Elijah reminds us to look forward to Heaven and to pray for the great day of Resurrection when the bodies of believers will be raised up to glory and reunited with their souls for all eternity!

Second, Elijah's ascension into Heaven teaches us that Heaven was a reality in the Old Testament. An error originated in the Middle Ages called limbus patrum (limbo of the fathers) that expressly denied the immediate entrance into Heaven for Old Testament believers. Instead, those Old Testament believers were locked up as it were in a dungeon (limbo) until Christ actually died in history, freed them from limbo, and brought them to Heaven.

The biblical reasons against this perspective are more than we can number and go beyond the purpose of this devotional, but suffice it to say this account of Elijah's entrance into heaven shows us no intermediate state in the Old Testament (beyond a swift whirlwind) before believers enter into glory.[1] In one verse, in a short period of time, Elijah, a sinner saved by the grace of God, was carried up in a chariot by a whirlwind, into heaven (vs. 11).

The promises of God are yes and amen. So certain are God's promises that even in the Old Testament Abraham could look forward by faith to the coming of Jesus and be saved by the blood of Christ shed 2,000 years later. So powerful is the blood of Christ that today you can look back in faith to the blood of Jesus Christ shed 2,000 years ago and be made righteous in the sight of God by the imputation of Christ's righteousness to you.

---

[1] Consider also Psalm 23:6: "Surely goodness and mercy shall follow me all the days of my life and I will dwell in the house of the Lord forever" and Psalm 73:24-25: "You will guide me with Your counsel, and afterward receive me to glory. Whom have I in heaven but You? And there is none upon earth that I desire besides You."

51

Elijah's Ascension, Part 5:
Concerning an Intermediate State or Purgatory in the New Testament

Then it happened, as they continued on and talked, that suddenly a chariot of fire appeared with horses of fire, and separated the two of them; and Elijah went up by a whirlwind into heaven.

II Kings 2:11 NKJV

In the prior chapter we considered glorification (the reunion of body and soul for all eternity with Christ) and the place of Heaven in the Old Testament. Today we will consider the third and final lesson.

Elijah's entrance into glory reminds us that our entrance into glory will be swift and that there is no intermediate state (such as purgatory) for the soul in the New Testament era. Jesus told the thief on the cross, "Assuredly, I say to you, today you will be with Me in paradise" (Luke 23:43).

The Roman Catholic doctrine of the intermediate state of purgatory between death and Heaven is a foreign concept to Scripture and must be rejected by believers and contended against for the salvation of those currently bound by the chains of Rome. I can think of no older and crueler, more horrible and soul crushing financial scheme than that of the Roman teaching on purgatory. Bernie Madoff could have only dreamed of such a program.

Purgatory is an old scheme in that it has been taught and monetized for well more than 500 years.

It is cruel in that it removes all sense, thought, or hope of assurance of salvation from God in this life. It binds the heart, soul, strength, and mind of men and women to the dungeon, toil, anguish, and chains of endless work and monetary payments to merit the mercy of God. This mercy can never be merited by man's works or money, making the pursuit of such impossibly cruel beyond my ability to detail.

It is cruel in that the doctrine is used to keep the souls of papists in constant fear of destruction, both in life and in death, and in need, not of Christ and His free grace and righteousness, but of the Roman Catholic Church and its doctrinal house of horror.

It is horrible for it creates a structure for followers where the only hope in the next life is hundreds, thousands, or more likely, millions of years in a hell-like state before the possibility of entrance into Heaven.[1]

It is a financial scheme in that people are told they can buy their way out of some but not all of purgatory and therefore gain Heaven for themselves or their relatives more quickly. The church assumes power over souls it does not have; sells promises from a

---

[1] See "Martin Luther" by Eric Metaxas, page 77. A tour of the relics just of Frederick's collection in Wittenberg could shave exactly 1,902,202 years and 270 days off of your time in purgatory. Of course no one knows the secret number of years souls supposedly stay in purgatory, so millions of years off is nothing if your allotted time is in the billions. Metaxas also outlines the business scheme of indulgences in the Middle Ages, showing it was as fine-tuned as any scheme in our present era. Lest we think that indulgences are a thing of the past, walk into a Roman Catholic Church and see about lighting a candle, having the priest dedicate a mass, or receiving the prayers of a certain monastic order. All of these things and more are available to you and your dead relatives... for a fee.

treasury of merit[2] that it does not control; promises escape from a horrible place of purgatory that does not exist; all while hiding the free gift of God in Christ that is freely offered to all who will turn to the Lord in faith.

Elijah's entrance into Heaven is of God's grace alone, through faith alone, not of Elijah's work, lest he should boast. There is no purgatory, an intermediate state; there is only Heaven for believers and hell for unbelievers. You cannot buy your way out of the one or into the other.

Roman Catholics may come to Jesus today without money but by faith in Christ and with repentance of sin and receive of Him eternal life. In Christ they will find that He alone is all sufficient to save. Nothing can be added to His work and nothing remains after His work that still needs to be accomplished. He did not almost accomplish salvation but accomplished salvation to the uttermost. Neither Mary, the saints, your relatives, nor you can help yourself into glory, but it is all of Christ who saves by His grace alone through faith alone. If you will take hold of Him by faith today you will receive everlasting life today!

---

[2] The Treasury of Merit is the supposed bank that the Pope controls and dispenses with as he pleases. According to the Roman Catholic Catechism it includes the infinite merit of Christ as well as *"the prayers and good works of the Blessed Virgin Mary. They are truly immense, unfathomable, and even pristine in their value before God. In the treasury, too, are the prayers and good works of all the saints, all those who have followed in the footsteps of Christ the Lord... In this way they attained their own salvation and at the same time cooperated in saving their brothers in the unity of the Mystical Body"* (Roman Catholic Catechism #1477). If Christ's merit is infinite what merit can Mary and the saints supposedly add? Logic like this has no place in idolatrous financial schemes and must not be asked inside Rome.

52

Great Loss and Great Gain

And Elisha saw it, and he cried out, "My father, my father, the chariot of Israel and its horsemen!" So he saw him no more. And he took hold of his own clothes and tore them into two pieces.

II Kings 2:12 NKJV

Which is better for a nation: to have the greatest, fiercest, most powerful army or to have the Lord? The psalmist said, "Some trust in chariots, and some in horses: but we will remember the name of the LORD our God" (Psalm 20:7). The fiercest warrior did little to assist the Philistines on the day a young shepherd went against him with a sling. So Israel with its weak armies found success only from the Lord. Elijah was to Israel like an army, a warrior, a general. He was the chariot (the captain), and he was the horsemen (the cavalry and strength of the army).

When Elijah ascended into Heaven a great loss came to Israel. Israel lost its prophet who had proclaimed over and over and against all persecution, that the Lord, He is God. They lost their prophet who had performed great miracles by the power of the Lord, even stopping the rain for three years and praying for fire to come down from Heaven. And now this man had left them and ascended into Heaven.

Elisha's relationship with Elijah was even closer, like that of a father and son. His cry and rending of his own clothes at the ascension of Elijah demonstrated the closeness of this younger prophet to the older. It reminds us of the relationship of Paul and Timothy and Moses and Joshua. There are those who taught us in the way of truth who have become like fathers to us, sometimes more so than our biological fathers because they showed us not only the way in this present world but also the way to the world to come.[1] For this, the cry is doubled, "My father, my father..."

When Jesus told His disciples He would depart from them in John 13:31-38, Peter expressed his desire to go with Jesus, that he would even lay down his life to follow Jesus. But Jesus would not allow it. Jesus went to prepare a place for His people and left them behind to carry out His work of making disciples of all nations. He also left His Spirit to be with them always.

When Elijah was taken up to Heaven, he was taken away from Israel. Israel had suffered a great loss. While few may have known it at the time, Israel's loss was also its gain, for the Lord had prepared another prophet to rise up in Elijah's place. Israel gained Elisha!

---

[1] "Jesus said to him, I am the way, the truth, and the life. No one comes to the Father except through Me" (John 14:6).

53

And Elisha Saw It! The Lord Answers Hard Prayers

And Elisha saw it, and he cried out, "My father, my father, the chariot of Israel and its horsemen!" So he saw him no more. And he took hold of his own clothes and tore them into two pieces.

II Kings 2:12 NKJV

When reading the Scripture out loud with my family, occasionally one of my boys will say something to me like, "Daddy, you are hurting my ears." This is not because they do not like the Scripture, in fact they often ask for more to be read. Rather, there are certain portions of Scripture I struggle to read at an appropriate volume. The passage builds up over many verses like a musical crescendo before reaching a climax at a triumphant declaration of the Lord's power, glory, name, or work. John 8:31 - 59 is one of those passages. Jesus was interacting with the Pharisees around many points concerning Abraham when near the end of that interaction they ask Him, "Are you greater than our father Abraham, who is dead?" (8:53). Jesus responded, "Your father Abraham rejoiced to see My day, and he saw it and was glad!"[1]

---

[1] Ancient Greek does not have exclamation points in it like modern Greek and English. It seems to me that this sentence ought to have an English exclamation point at the end of it rather than a period. However, please note that most English translations use a period, so this is a deviation from the English translation to seek to highlight the majesty of the words and truth that Jesus spoke in these verses. An exclamation point should be used at the end of vs. 58 as well!

The unity of the Old and New Testament faith, the deity of Christ, the hope of salvation, are all declared in one small verse. It is among the greatest interactions recorded for us of Jesus's earthly ministry. Abraham rejoiced to see the day of Jesus, and he saw it!

With the drama of the events unfolding around Elijah's ascension into Heaven and Elisha's passionate mourning at the loss of his spiritual father, we must remember to focus on the first four words of verse twelve, which set the stage for the rest of Elisha's life on earth. "And Elisha saw it..."

What did Elisha see? He saw the chariot and horses of fire bring Elijah up by a whirlwind into Heaven. He saw Elijah's mantle fall to the ground. He saw the sky close up so that his father was with him no more.

Why does it matter that Elisha saw it? Before Elijah was taken up from earth he asked Elisha what he could do for him before he was taken away (vs 9), and Elisha asked for a double portion of Elijah's spirit.

The spirit of Elijah was not Elijah's to give away, for it was the spirit of the Lord. Who could give such a thing in any portion (let alone, double portion) but the Lord Himself? So Elijah told Elisha that he had asked for "a hard thing" (vs. 10). Nevertheless, if Elisha saw Elijah when he was taken up into Heaven, it would mean the Lord had given Elisha the double portion. If Elisha did not see it meant the Lord had not given it. "And Elisha saw it..." The Lord was with Elisha. The Lord was with Israel. The Lord is always with His people. Elisha asked a hard thing. He asked a great thing. He asked for the Spirit of the Lord that was with Elijah to be with him and the Lord granted his request.

Brothers and sisters, are you asking hard things of the Lord? We need to take encouragement from the Word when we pray and ask hard things of the Lord. Who knows the Lord's mind and will as to His answer? Are we praying for one new family to join the church this year? Keep praying for that family and that the Lord would fill the building with true worshipers in all faithful churches this year. Are we praying for the weakening of particular sins in ourselves? Let us pray for the death of those sins also! Are we praying for the end of surgical abortion? Let us also pray for the end of all abortion! Are we praying for NAPARC churches to hold the biblical line in areas like marriage and sexuality? Let us also pray for righteousness to abound in our congregations! Are we praying for our children to embrace Christ by faith? Let us also pray they would serve Christ and His bride all their days without reservation!

Let us go boldly before the throne of God with confidence, as children to a father, asking Him who made Heaven and Earth to do hard things for us. Then we, like Elisha and Abraham, will be able to say, "And we saw it!"

54

Taking Up The Mantle

He also took up the mantle of Elijah that had fallen from him, and went back and stood by the bank of the Jordan.

II Kings 2:13 NKJV

There are some phrases and concepts from Scripture that have been so thoroughly absorbed into English usage that those who use them today often have little knowledge of their biblical origin or meaning. Believers and unbelievers alike may refer to a "scapegoat" (Leviticus 16); "A drop in the bucket" (Isaiah 40:15); the "writing on the wall" (Daniel 5); or a "surety" (Gen. 43:9, Heb. 7:22).

When a younger person takes up the work of an older person or a protege continues the work of a mentor, another biblical phrase is often used: He "took up the mantle." When Elijah was taken into the chariot of fire, his mantle fell from him and Elisha took it up. The meaning we associate with the phrase today had the same original meaning in the Scripture. Elisha was taking up and continuing the work the Lord had called Elijah to do.

The Lord took one prophet to glory and set up another prophet to continue revealing the Word of the Lord to Israel. Elisha did not wait to take up the work: he took up the mantle immediately and returned to the Jordan River. The mantle that was once thrown over him (I Kings 19:19) was now taken up as a sign that the spirit of Elijah was upon him and that he was the successor of Elijah when there were perhaps no other witnesses to his divine anointing.[1]

Who will continue your work for the Lord when you are called to glory? If you are an elderly woman, faithfully praying for the church and her labor of proclaiming, promoting, and protecting the truth, who will be praying for such things when you are with the saints triumphant in the throne room of King Jesus? Will you teach younger women now of your prayers and practices that they may be well prepared to take up your mantle when you ride the chariot and horses of fire to Heaven? If you are a church officer, missionary, or theologian, are you preparing the next generation of men to take up the Lord's work that you will be leaving behind? How will you prepare them to take it up with double the focus that you were able to give?

Whose work will you take up in service for the King? If you are that young woman learning from the older woman, are you practicing prayer and implementing those practices that have so helped Christ's church for millennia? If you are a younger minister or considering full-time ministry in the church, are you preparing to plant the seeds and water the fields that others have plowed? Service in the church is not always new, groundbreaking service but much of the time is simply taking up the mantle of those who have labored in front of us until the Lord returns and brings in the harvest.

---

[1] The Lord gives signs to remind us of His glorious names, titles, attributes, Word, and works. Neither Elisha, the sons of the prophets, nor anyone else we read about in II Kings ever worshiped Elijah's mantle. Many did worship other objects in history such as the bronze serpent and to some extent the ark of the covenant, but those who did so were sinning. The practice in Roman Catholicism of venerating / worshiping relics is giving glory that is properly reserved for the Lord God alone, to a created object. Venerating relics is idolatry. Kissing a box holding the supposedly still-beating heart of a dead saint is idolatry no different from the pagan religions we see dominating other countries of the world.

Service for the Kingdom is a great labor. It is our first and highest calling: "Seek ye first the kingdom of God..." It is not necessarily a glamorous calling. It is not necessarily a visible calling. Some labor in the church no one will see but you and the Lord. Most of your prayers will never be heard by others. The world would question the point of such activity when there is no one nearby to "like" it. There may not be financial compensation. It may be wearisome. It may be heartbreaking. In many places today it is dangerous labor, perhaps deadly. But what a glorious thing to be even a doorkeeper in the house of the Lord. Take up the mantle of those who have gone before you and labor on!

> *Go labor on; spend, and be spent,*
> *Thy joy to do the Father's will;*
> *It is the way the Master went;*
> *Should not the servant tread it still?*
>
> ~Horatius Bonar

55

Where is the Lord God of Elijah?

Then he took the mantle of Elijah that had fallen from him, and struck the water, and said, "Where is the LORD God of Elijah?" And when he also had struck the water, it was divided this way and that; and Elisha crossed over.

II Kings 2:14 NKJV

Earlier this year I met a man who told me he bought a Maserati. The only problem was it had been totaled in an accident and, in addition to significant body damage, its engine had been destroyed. He had a Maserati but it was of very little use without an engine.

Elisha had the mantle of Elijah. With this mantle the other prophets would recognize the succession of the office. But Elisha knew that the mantle of Elijah was of no help if the God of Elijah was not also with him. It was not the might of Elijah that caused the oil to last for the widow throughout the famine. It was not the strength of Elijah that raised the widow's son from the dead or called fire down from Heaven on Carmel or on the captains and their fifties who came to take him. It was the Lord God of Elijah who did these great deeds through His servant. As Elisha returned to the Jordan he prayed for the Lord God of Elijah to be with him as He was with Elijah.

Today we have many treasures even greater than the mantle of Elijah. We have the whole Scripture at our fingertips, not a mere portion of the Old Testament on rare scrolls. We have the faithful preaching of the Word in nearly every city in America and in most countries around the world. We have sermons in abundance, catechisms, creeds, and great writings from the church fathers. We have all these things and yet if we do not have the Lord God of Elijah we have nothing.

Elisha's attention was not on the mantle in his hands but immediately on the Lord and with that great need, he cried out to the Lord in prayer. The Lord God of Elijah was with Elisha and would be for the remainder of his life. As you face the labors and trials of life are you calling on the Lord God of Elijah today or trusting in the mantle of a prophet? We have many privileges 2,000 years after the ascension of Jesus Christ. Nevertheless, we still need the Lord God of Elijah to be with us or we have nothing. Cry out to Him while He still may be found![1]

---

[1] If you would like to read further on this prayer of Elisha at the Jordan river, I would highly encourage reading Charles Spurgeon's sermon on this text: https://www.spurgeon.org/resource-library/sermons/where-is-the-god-of-elijah#flipbook/ .

56

This Way and That: The Lord Divides the Jordan

Then he took the mantle of Elijah that had fallen from him, and struck the water, and said, "Where is the LORD God of Elijah?" And when he also had struck the water, it was divided this way and that; and Elisha crossed over.

II Kings 2:14 NKJV

Sometimes when reading the Scripture regularly it is possible to glance over great miracles of the Lord because Scripture is so full of miracles. Take Deuteronomy 29:5 for example: "I have led you forty years in the wilderness. Your clothes have not worn out on you, and your sandals have not worn out on your feet..." Did you catch that? For forty years, more than of two million pairs of sandals and as many or more garments did not wear out! Amazing provision of the Lord.

By the time we reach II Kings 2:14, the Jordan has already been divided once (2:9) and then it is divided again. The way the Lord describes this miracle in both verses is among the great understatements of Scripture: "It was divided this way and that." Today the Jordan River is more than 200 miles long. When Elisha prayed to the Lord and struck the river with Elijah's mantle, the Lord parted the river so that some of the water went one way, the rest of the water went the other way, and Elisha crossed over on dry land.

Nearly every chapter of Elijah's and Elisha's lives involves a miracle of some type taking place, and it can be tempting to pass over them quickly, however, we should meditate on this great division of the Jordan River. This was the same river, and the same direction, by which the Israelites first entered the Promised Land many hundreds of years earlier. The Lord used the same method of bringing Elisha back into Israel where he would no longer be the one who served Elijah but the prophet who served God's people.

Why did God perform this miracle? For at least three reasons: 1) So that Elisha would be assured that the Lord God of Elijah was indeed with him; 2) So that the sons of the prophets would see and could testify that the spirit of Elijah was with Elisha; and 3) so that we would know that the Lord is with all those who call upon Him in truth.

Jesus did many miracles during His earthly ministry. Their quantity makes the miracles of Elisha and Elijah seem few. Why did Jesus perform these miracles? To show His power? Certainly that was a part. But there was a particular focus: to show to all the world that the Son of Man, Jesus Christ, had power on earth to forgive sins (Mark 2:10-11)! Lest anyone doubt the authority of the Savior to save, He told a paralytic man to stand up, take up his bed, and go to his house.

God's dividing the Jordan demonstrated to Israel that Elisha came with the authority of the Lord. His message was not his own but the Lord's. The Lord testified to this with great miracles through Elisha, beginning with moving the Jordan this way and that so that His servant might pass through.

As we read of the miracles performed by God through Elisha in the coming pages of Scripture, may we not glance over them. May we rather remember that the God who moved the Jordan this way and that, who caused millions of sandals to remain unscathed for 40 years, who raised the paralytic, who rose from the dead and ascended, this God, He is our God forever and ever. He will be our guide even through death (Psalm 4:14)!

57

Where Should We Search?

Now when the sons of the prophets who were from Jericho saw him, they said, "The spirit of Elijah rests on Elisha." And they came to meet him, and bowed to the ground before him. Then they said to him, "Look now, there are fifty strong men with your servants. Please let them go and search for your master, lest perhaps the Spirit of the LORD has taken him up and cast him upon some mountain or into some valley." And he said, "You shall not send anyone." But when they urged him till he was ashamed, he said, "Send them!" Therefore they sent fifty men, and they searched for three days but did not find him. And when they came back to him, for he had stayed in Jericho, he said to them, "Did I not say to you, 'Do not go'?"

II Kings 2:15-18 NKJV

What is truth? Since the fall of Adam when Satan twisted the truth of God into a lie, mankind has been missing the truth and believing lies. In our current times, rather than outrightly denying truth, people refer to "my truth" and "your truth" (two different ideas), as if that which is true can change from person to person. In contrast, Christianity teaches that truth is an objective reality rather than subjective opinion. It is a person Jesus Christ: "I am the way, the truth, and the life..." (John 14:6). It is the Word of God, the Scriptures of the Old and New Testaments, the Bible: "Thy Word is truth" (John 17:17). It is unchanging: "...The word of our God shall stand forever" (Isaiah 40:8). And yet sometimes it is difficult for Christians to submit to the truth, so they look elsewhere.

This was the case for the sons of the prophets in Jericho. They had directly received the word of God (2:5) that Elijah would be taken away. But after Elisha returned alone and these men recognized him as the spiritual successor of Elijah, they wanted to go look for their friend and leader in the mountains and valleys. As a hiker who regularly hears the mountains calling, I am sympathetic to the fifty men desiring to engage in this trek. However, Elisha the prophet said, "You shall not go" (2:16). They had the prophecy of the Lord and the word of the prophet, but they still wanted to search for Elijah and eventually Elisha relented.

For three days, fifty men searched the mountains and valleys for Elijah in case the Lord dropped him out of the chariot: they, of course, did not find him for the Lord had brought him to Heaven as He had told the prophets and as Elisha witnessed. When the fifty returned, Elisha gently reprimanded them, "Did I not say to you, do not go?" Often a gentle rebuke will have great reward in the godly who receive it as did these sons of the prophets (Proverbs 3:11-12).

It can be tempting for us not to accept the Word of God. Even though we read the Word and hear it preached by faithful ministers, perhaps we still want to search elsewhere for the truth. Many in the church seem to be always searching for the truth but never coming to the knowledge of it. They search in the mountains and valleys of the world's wisdom. Rather than relenting after three days, they are given over to new ideas and teachings, to the instability of their families and the grief of the church.

As Elisha took up the mantle of Elijah and began the new chapter of service to the Lord, he began by reminding the prophets of the confidence they must have in the truth of God's Word. It took patience and a few days of waiting, but the prophets learned to trust the Lord and rely on Him for truth. Without reliance on the Word of God, there is no gospel, there is no salvation, there is no hope. With the infallible and inerrant Word as our guide, life, hope, and salvation are found for us in Christ Jesus.

Let us take two foundational lessons with us today: 1) Have confidence in the God of truth and rest in Him and His Word of truth. In so doing you have the foundation from where you may grow in the grace and knowledge of the Lord and will not be ashamed when you see Him appear. 2) Do not be a witness to your truth or my truth, but to the Truth. This confused and rebellious age is always searching for the truth and ends up delighting in lies. If you stand for the truth, you will be mocked and hated by many, but you may also be the means of delivering the light to some who are in darkness.

58

An Aroma of Life, Part 1: The Situation

Then the men of the city said to Elisha, "Please notice, the situation of this city is pleasant, as my lord sees; but the water is bad, and the ground barren." And he said, "Bring me a new bowl, and put salt in it." So they brought it to him. Then he went out to the source of the water, and cast in the salt there, and said, "Thus says the LORD: 'I have healed this water; from it there shall be no more death or barrenness.' So the water remains healed to this day, according to the word of Elisha which he spoke.

II Kings 2:19-22 NKJV

There have been many debates as to the best method for evangelism. On one extreme of the debate, some have taken the position we should only warn of judgment, as Jonah who told Nineveh it would be destroyed. Those on the other extreme focus solely on the love of God, even going so far as to tell everyone in earshot that God loves him and has a wonderful plan for his life. Many are somewhere in between these two positions.

I do not anticipate that a simple devotional will settle the question once and for all.[1] But one thing is certain: The faithful proclamation of the gospel will be an aroma of death leading to death for some and an aroma of life leading to life for others (II Cor. 2:12-16). Not all who hear your reason for the hope that is within you will believe you.

What do the gospel and evangelism have to do with Elisha and the water at Jericho? Jericho was a city cursed by God when it was destroyed by Joshua and the Israelites. Whoever rebuilt it would

---

[1] It seems to me the specific individual's situation is the primary determination for which evangelistic approach to take.

lose two sons (Joshua 6:26) and in the days of Ahab, Hiel of Bethel[2] rebuilt Jericho at the expense of two of his sons' lives (I Kings 16:34).

However, there was no sin in living in the rebuilt city, and in fact it had become one of the training centers of the prophets. Elijah visited to encourage the prophets before he was taken up to Heaven and Elisha spent some time with the men before he departed for other places of ministry. The setting of Jericho was pleasant, but the water was bad and therefore the ground was barren. Nothing could grow from the water that was available.[3] Food and water had to be constantly shipped in from other places to keep the residents alive. There was no life sustaining food from Jericho itself.

The Lord used the picture of water with the Samaritan woman in John 4. She was at a well when He told her about the living water. She had water she could drink, but she would thirst again. She needed living water - water that would become a fountain springing up to everlasting life. In comparison, all other water would eventually lead to death.

We may live in pleasant places and situations with abundant water to drink. Yet the places we live, our neighborhoods, towns, states, and countries are dead without the living water. The bad water of Jericho reminded the prophets and should remind us that the present situation may seem pleasant, but the end thereof is only death. Every man, woman, and child now living will one day perish, and unless the Lord heals us and gives to us living water our pleasant situation will end in misery and destruction.

---

[2] Bethel had been a city of great idolatry and wickedness since the days of Jeroboam, who caused Israel to sin. It should be no surprise the man who rebuilt Jericho at the known cost of his two sons was from Bethel.

[3] It seems unlikely the water was drinkable, though the text focuses on the effect on crops rather than the potability of the water.

The prophets who would spread the Word of God, Christians who will bear witness to the truth, must begin with this recognition of the situation: The water of the world is bad, the land is barren, the end thereof is the way of death. But the Lord, by His grace and mercy, provides a remedy!

59

An Aroma of Life, Part 2: The Remedy

Then the men of the city said to Elisha, "Please notice, the situation of this city is pleasant, as my lord sees; but the water is bad, and the ground barren." And he said, "Bring me a new bowl, and put salt in it." So they brought it to him. Then he went out to the source of the water, and cast in the salt there, and said, "Thus says the LORD: 'I have healed this water; from it there shall be no more death or barrenness.' So the water remains healed to this day, according to the word of Elisha which he spoke.

II Kings 2:19-22 NKJV

My family and I were recently driving to a store and in the parking lot we saw two women and four children holding signs. One said, "For all have sinned and fallen short of the glory of God" (Rom 3:23). Another sign read, "For the wages of sin is death..." (Rom 6:23a). That was the spiritual situation in Jericho more than 2,500 years ago, as it is in the world today. Death. Can that which is dead ever be made alive? Can poisonous water become good water? Can dry bones live? Naturally speaking, the answer is no.

When this question was posed to the prophet Ezekiel he did not answer based on his knowledge of nature but answered based on his knowledge of God who created and sustains all nature: "O Lord God, you know" (Ezekiel 37:3). After Ezekiel prophesied to the bones and the Lord who freely works above nature (supernaturally) gave them life, the Lord said, " I will put My Spirit in you, and you shall live..." (37:14).

The situation around Jericho was poisonous water and a dead land. The same spiritual situation is around us. But the Lord provides a remedy through two means: 1) His Word; and 2) His Spirit.

"Thus says the Lord: "I have healed this water; from it there shall be no more death or barrenness" (2:20). As Ezekiel would do in the valley some years later, Elisha did at Jericho. He proclaimed the Word of the Lord, the source of truth. This is the same work the faithful minister conducts each Lord's Day worship service: proclaiming the Word of the Lord. He pours in the salt (2:20-21; Matthew 5:13). By God's Word the message will go out.

By God's Spirit, the message is effectual and takes root in the souls of sinners. "So the water remains healed to this day" (2:22). The water at Jericho was never poisonous again. Those who have Christ as their Lord and Savior have the living water and will never thirst again. We must bring forth fruit for the King who gave us life abundantly.

The world is looking for a remedy for the sin and seeming madness around us in the form of viruses, violence, and vengeance. What is the remedy for this barren situation?

The third sign held by the ladies in the parking lot completed Rom 6:23, "...but the gift of God is eternal life in Christ Jesus our Lord." There was a deadly situation in Jericho as there is around us today, but there was and is a remedy. It is the gospel: eternal life and salvation in, by, and through Christ Jesus our Lord. Jesus died in our place and for our sins that we might not die but have everlasting life. To those who are being saved, this gospel of Jesus Christ is a sweet smelling aroma. What could be sweeter than Jesus who saves? Repent and believe in Him!

60

An Aroma of Death: 42 Children and 2 Bears

Then he went up from there to Bethel; and as he was going up the road, some youths came from the city and mocked him, and said to him, "Go up, you baldhead! Go up, you baldhead!" So he turned around and looked at them, and pronounced a curse on them in the name of the LORD. And two female bears came out of the woods and mauled forty-two of the youths.

Then he went from there to Mount Carmel, and from there he returned to Samaria.

II Kings 2:23-25 NKJV

I f you were to think of particularly evil times in biblical history, what would come to mind? Perhaps the time of Noah when the sin of men led to God destroying the earth with a flood? Perhaps the rampant homosexuality at Sodom and Gomorrah that resulted in destruction of whole cities with fire and brimstone from heaven? Perhaps the early days of King Manasseh of Judah who caused his son to be burned in fire? Perhaps the days of Ahab who did worse than all the kings of Israel before him when all but 7,000 in Israel bowed the knee to Baal? Usually we think of the horrible blasphemy and wicked practices of adults throughout history who have sinned against the Lord. I suspect we rarely think about children committing some of the more heinous sins in biblical history.

The closing verses of II Kings 2 paint for us the totality of the rebellion of Israel against God in the days of Elisha and the mind of God as it relates to sin. The youths, the children of Israel, were wholly given over to blasphemy and mockery of God and His prophets. Elisha was retracing the final visits of Elijah (Jordan River to Jericho to Bethel) when he approached Bethel, and children came out of the city to mock him.

It can be tempting with this text to think the punishment was unequal to the crime of innocent young children. But listen to their words, "Go up, you bald head! Go up, you bald head!" (Vs. 23). It is evident the children had heard the prophecy or the account of Elijah's ascension (going up) to Heaven. Like their kings, they hated Elijah and were glad to see him go, though they likely doubted the manner of his leaving. So they told Elisha to go up the way of Elijah. They were in essence saying, "Leave us! Leave us, you who think Elijah was carried up to Heaven by your God! We despise and reject such prophecies, but if it were true, you should go too, you bald head."

Like the two captains consumed with their men when blaspheming God's prophet in chapter 1, these children were not simply mocking Elisha's bald spot, they were mocking the God of Elisha, your God! They mocked God's miracle of taking Elijah to glory. They mocked God's Spirit that anointed Elisha. They mocked God's comfort to a dead land in the form of a living prophet. They mocked even his physical imperfections.

In light of this blasphemy of the Lord, Elisha, in the name of the Lord pronounced judgment and a curse on the children. Immediately two female bears came out of the woods, as if robbed of their young and fiercely mauled forty-two children of Bethel.

The joyful ascension of Elijah to glory, the provision of the Lord in the prophet Elisha, the healing of the bad water at Jericho, the proclamation of the glory of God and salvation in Him was a delightful sweet aroma and salvation to some. To others, even these children, the glorious gospel was an aroma of death, even a thing to be mocked, and it led only to destruction.

This passage should rightly put the fear of the Lord before us and remind us that God will not be mocked. If God will judge little children from ancient Israel in such a manner for their wickedness, how much more will he judge us? He will judge the wicked of all ages and likewise He will show mercy on all those who repent of their wicked sins and embrace Jesus Christ who is freely offered to us in the gospel.

61

Mountain Memories

Then he went from there to Mount Carmel, and from there he returned to Samaria.

II Kings 2:23-25 NKJV

Mountains play a prominent role in Scripture. Jesus's longest sermon took place on a mountain (Matt. 5-7). Often when Jesus went to pray, He did so after going up a mountain (Matt. 14:23). Jesus was transfigured at the top of a mountain (Matt. 17:1). The law was given on Mount Sinai. And one of the greatest public manifestations of the Lord's glory above the worthlessness of idols took place on Mount Carmel.

After Elisha witnessed the effect of the gospel ministry, an aroma of life for some and an aroma of death for others, he made his way back to Samaria but not before going to Mount Carmel. These days it is something of a trend for ministers and theologians to write and teach about the need for vacations and rest. While the Lord does give His people rest at appropriate times, I am not sure Americans need this exhortation quite so frequently when we spend on average five hours per day watching television. Nevertheless, mountains can be a place of great refreshment, even if we are only there briefly. We are not told that Elisha took physical rest at Mount Carmel but only that he went there en route to Samaria.

Mount Carmel was a memorial for Elisha, for it was there that God revealed Himself so gloriously through His servant Elijah with fire from heaven. Perhaps after the terrible destruction of the scornful children, the refreshment of being at that mountain of the Lord strengthened Elisha for his further service to the Lord. We are not told what Elisha did there, but we know the mountain was a memorial to the fact that the Lord, He is God. As you once again reflect on the work of the Lord at Mount Carmel, consider other great mountains that you have seen in pictures or in person and consider the words of Psalm 36:6: "Your righteousness is like the great mountains..." The God whose righteousness is beyond our comprehension is our God. Let us abide with Him forever and ever for He will be our guide even unto death (Psalm 48:14).

62

A Tale of Two Evils

Now Jehoram the son of Ahab became king over Israel at Samaria in the eighteenth year of Jehoshaphat king of Judah, and reigned twelve years. And he did evil in the sight of the LORD, but not like his father and mother; for he put away the sacred pillar of Baal that his father had made. Nevertheless he persisted in the sins of Jeroboam the son of Nebat, who had made Israel sin; he did not depart from them.

II Kings 3:1-3 NKJV

Which would you rather have attack you, a grizzly or a wolf? For me, both sound terrible, but if I had to choose I would take the wolf as I would have more of a fighting chance. In hypotheticals like this we often consider which is the lesser of two evils.

After Jehoram's introduction at the beginning of II Kings 3, we are brought up to speed on his life before the Lord through a comparison to Ahab, the most evil king in Israel's history. Jehoram was evil, but he was less evil than Ahab and Jezebel. Since Jeroboam it seemed each king of Israel was more evil than the preceding king... but Ahab was too tough to beat in the category of evil.

We should not take this passage as a commendation of Jehoram: to the contrary this passage gives us another indictment against the evil of Ahab and Jezebel. Jehoram's prevailing sin was idolatry. He put away the pillar to Baal, but he did not end Baal worship or idolatry in Israel; rather he just focused his idolatry on the sin of

Jeroboam.[1] Jehoram, like his fathers Ahab and Jeroboam, "exchanged the truth of God for a lie, and worshiped and served the creature rather than the Creator, who is blessed forever" (Romans 1:25).

This is the prevailing sin throughout history, and our present day is no different. If I lust after the desires of my eyes, the desires of my flesh, or the pride of life, I am making those things my gods who save me rather than the true and living triune God, who alone saves through His atoning work on the cross for me. I would be committing idolatry like Jeroboam, Ahab, and Jehoram if I were to look anywhere else for hope but to Christ my savior.

Today, the people of the nations are falling down to the idols of pride, greed, vengeance, violence, deceit, bodily autonomy[2], and all manner of similar idols. The corporations, politicians, and all of world seem to be following their example. As the Lord looks down from Heaven would He say we are less evil than any other generation before us?

Jehoram persisted in the sins of Jeroboam. Those who claim the Word of God as the infallible and inerrant Word of God; who claim Jesus Christ as the Son of God and God the Son; who boast in the cross of Christ: Let us persist, not in doing every evil deed, but

---

[1] Jeroboam's sin is given in I Kings 12:28-31: "Therefore the king [Jeroboam] asked advice, made two calves of gold, and said to the people, "It is too much for you to go up to Jerusalem. Here are your gods, O Israel, which brought you up from the land of Egypt!" And he set up one in Bethel, and the other he put in Dan. Now this thing became a sin, for the people went to worship before the one as far as Dan. He made shrines on the high places, and made priests from every class of people, who were not the sons of Levi."

[2] Bodily autonomy (Perhaps it can be referred to as the idol "Botonomy" for short) is the prevailing idol of our day and the false god by whom all manner of wickedness and sin is justified. We will see the results of Botonomy worship playing out throughout this chapter of Scripture and culminating in the final verse. It is very much like what we are seeing in the present day.

dying to sin, evil, and idolatry and living for the glory and honor of Christ. Then, dear friends, as you by the Spirit persist in righteousness and live for the glory of Christ, others will see your good works and glorify your Father in Heaven.

63

King Mesha and the Moabites

Now Mesha king of Moab was a sheepbreeder, and he regularly paid the king of Israel one hundred thousand lambs and the wool of one hundred thousand rams. But it happened, when Ahab died, that the king of Moab rebelled against the king of Israel.

II Kings 3:4-5 NKJV

What do Eglon, Balak, and Mesha have in common? They were all kings of Moab.[1] Moab has a long and well chronicled history in the Bible. The father of the Moabites was Moab, the son of Lot's oldest daughter who committed great sin with her father after the destruction of Sodom and Gomorrah.[2] The Moabites played a role in the wandering of the Israelites in the wilderness before they entered the Promised Land. King Balak desired to curse Israel through Balaam his sorcerer, only to have Israel blessed and Moab eventually destroyed (though not before Israel's men sinned with Moabite women).

After Israel entered the Promised Land, Joshua died and the Israelites rebelled against the Lord by worshipping the abominations (false gods) of the nations surrounding them. The Moabites ruled over Israel with a heavy hand multiple times in Judges as Israel rebelled against God. During the days of Saul, Israel was constantly warring with surrounding nations, the Moabites, Ammonites, and Philistines but in the days of King David, the Moabites were subdued and became servants of Israel

---

[1] See Judges 3:14 (Eglon); Numbers 22 (Balak); and II Kings 3:4 (Mesha).
[2] Genesis 19:37.

and King David. Nevertheless, Solomon built a high place in Israel for Chemosh, the abomination of Moab, and for Molech, the abomination of Ammon (I Kings 11:7), which caused Solomon and all Israel to sin. Throughout the history of the kings of Israel and Judah the Moabites were a constant military enemy and the god(s) of Moab were a constant evil temptation causing Israel to commit idolatry. Moab's wickedness in Scripture is directly tied to its false gods and the Lord devotes nearly two whole chapters in Isaiah (15 & 16) to tell of its utter destruction.

It was during the days of Ahab that the Moabites were either defeated or formed an alliance / treaty with Israel under the terms of which Moab paid Israel 100,000 lambs and the wool of 100,000 rams each year. In Ahab's day, it seemed Moab had its eye on Judah and was focused on destroying king Jehoshaphat, which of course it was not able to do (II Chron. 20). But when Ahab died, Mesha broke the treaty and rebelled against Jehoram, King of Israel. This is the political context in II Kings 3.

However, by the grace of God, we do not need to end this devotional regarding the Moabites only in terms of Moabite abominations. While abominations were the memorial of Moab, the Lord has His remnant among all nations, tribes, and tongues. At the end of the time of the Judges, some Israelites went to live in Moab, including a man named Elimelech from Bethlehem-Judah and his family. He and his two sons died in Moab but not before both his sons married Moabite women, one of whom was named Ruth. Ruth married Boaz and gave birth to Obed, the father of Jesse, the father of King David. Directly in the family line of Jesus Christ was none other than a Moabite whose name titles one of the 66 books of the Bible.

Yes, the Moabites were wholly given to sin and all manner of abominations, little different from our present day. But sin and evil cannot hinder Christ's glorious work of salvation, for He saved Ruth the Moabite and used her mightily in His kingdom.

64

An Unusual Alliance

*So King Jehoram went out of Samaria at that time and mustered
all Israel. Then he went and sent to Jehoshaphat king of Judah,
saying, "The king of Moab has rebelled against me. Will you go
with me to fight against Moab?" And he said, "I will go up; I am as
you are, my people as your people, my horses as your horses."
Then he said, "Which way shall we go up?" And he answered, "By
way of the Wilderness of Edom." So the king of Israel went with
the king of Judah and the king of Edom, and they marched on that
roundabout route seven days; and there was no water for the
army, nor for the animals that followed them.*

II Kings 3:6-9 NKJV

One of the greatest events in military history is an account
unlikely to be found in any military college, officer's
training course, or textbook on strategy for military
success. It is the account in II Chronicles 20 of the armies of Moab,
Ammon, and Mt. Seir coming to destroy Jehoshaphat and the
nation of Judah. After praying to God for help and all of Judah
worshipping the Lord, the army of Judah, small in comparison to
the innumerable company coming against them, went out with
singing led by the Levites. The Lord caused the three armies
opposing Judah to fight amongst themselves so that when Judah
arrived they could simply gather the spoils of war. The Lord fought
for Judah and gave the people rest from their enemies.

With the rebellion of Moab against Israel, Jehoram was putting
together an alliance to bring the Moabites back under his control.
He first went to Jehoshaphat who had aligned himself with Ahab
and with Ahaziah in military and business ventures. Jehoshaphat

quickly aligned himself with Israel yet again as Jehoram desired to go fight against Moab. Edom would be brought into the pact after Jehoshaphat.

From the examples of Jehoshaphat's other alliances with Israel, we should learn that Jehoshaphat should not have gone to war on the side of Israel or Edom. The Lord had given great victories to Judah in the past and help from other nations, namely those opposed to the Lord, was not needed. Nevertheless, all three nations had issues with Moab. Israel, Edom, and Judah all bordered Moab, and Judah had recently been invaded by Moab in an attempt to destroy it. So all three nations had reason to desire the destruction of Moab, which had signaled war by not paying tribute.

If you look at the map of Israel in the time of the kings you will note that Moab is situated directly opposite Judah across the Dead Sea. The typical way of entry into Moab from Judah or vice versa was the friendly northern terrain, into the land of Ammon and across the Jordan River. This was how Moab, Ammon, and Mt. Seir came against Jerusalem so quickly in II Chron. 20 because they came from the Northern route with limited warning. The longer route was through the wilderness of Edom south of Judah and then North into Moab. The danger of this route was the inhospitable wilderness in the south, which could lead travelers many days without food or water. It was unlikely for a great army to travel this route, so Moab did not anticipate an attack from this direction and did not strengthen its defenses.

This dangerous southern route was the way chosen by Jehoram, agreed to by Jehoshaphat, and consented to by the king of Edom, a surprise attack on Moab from the south (farthest from Israel). Into the wilderness the armies went for seven days and found neither food nor water to replenish their stores. In one week, the optimistic allies went from preparing a surprise attack on Edom to being on the brink of destruction by the elements.

Our help does not come from wisdom or strategy, strength of arms, or will to succeed. Our help comes from the Lord. He who fought so wonderfully for Judah was able to cause a great army of mighty men to lay waste in the wilderness or to succeed in battle. As we go about our goals, work, and duties of the day, may we not stumble foolishly in our own craftiness because we forgot the Lord, but may we remember the Lord and bring glory to Jesus Christ our Savior by seeking first His Kingdom and righteousness in all that we do.

65

The Mutability and Fear of Idolaters

And the king of Israel said, "Alas! For the LORD has called these three kings together to deliver them into the hand of Moab."

II Kings 3:10 NKJV

Paul and Barnabas were in Lystra one day when they met a man who was crippled from birth. Paul, seeing the man had faith to be healed, told him to stand up on his feet. He did so and leaped and walked. When the people of Lystra heard this they believed their idols to have come down to them in the likeness of men. They praised Paul as Hermès and Barnabas as Zeus. They were ready to make sacrifices to them and would have but for the pleading of Paul and Barnabas to worship God. Then Jews from Antioch and Iconium came and persuaded the multitude to stone Paul. Suddenly the man they thought was Hermès incarnate was deemed worthy of death and stoning.[1]

When Jesus was beginning His earthly ministry He preached to the people the word of God from the prophecy of Isaiah. The people marveled at Jesus when He told them the Scripture was fulfilled on that very day. But when Jesus warned them about rejecting Him and not inheriting the promise of Abraham, the people were filled with wrath and set about to throw Jesus off a cliff. The one whom they marveled one minute they sought to kill the next minute, but Jesus passed safely through the midst of them.[2]

When the food and water were low and hope was all but lost for the armies of Judah, Israel, and Edom, the idol worshipping king of Israel gave up his hope of a week earlier and decided that rather

---

[1] Acts 14

[2] Luke 4:14-30

than destroy Moab, they would all certainly die. This is the mutability of idolaters and all those apart from the Lord. They can praise a man one moment and be ready to stone him the next. They have no secure foundation so they drift in every which direction and in great fear.

Jehoram would not worship the true and the living God. He served the golden calves of Jeroboam. Now in his hour of need, he confessed the LORD, not as Savior, protector, or King, but as the one who will rightly judge the world for its sin. Jehoram expressed something in this one verse that the world often does today but does not recognize. Jehoram acknowledged the God he desired only to suppress and deny as he thought he saw his end drawing near. What a terrible state for a soul. No foundation, given always to changing beliefs, and in the end still confessing the Lord but only as the dreadful judge and not as Savior.

Think about the way the world uses the name of "God" or "Jesus Christ" so often in a blasphemous and vain way. But even as they do that, they are acknowledging the truth that there is indeed a God and He will rightly judge them for their sin because while they knew God, they did not glorify Him as God, but suppressed the truth of God in unrighteousness.[3]

If you are reading this devotional today and have neither received Christ nor rested and trusted in Him alone for salvation as He is freely offered in the gospel, this fate of Jehoram is inevitably your fate. When fear comes upon you, none will help you. When the end is near, none will be with you. The Lord God you have denied will still be there but only to pronounce a just sentence of eternal death and hell fire upon you for your sin. All the idols and lies you pursued in your life will be nowhere to be found. Bodily Autonomy, Critical Race Theory, the LGBTQ+ community, Allah, the Book of Mormon, the Watchtower Society, the Pope, Mary, your

---

[3] See Romans 1 especially verses 18-32

money - none of it will help you in the hour of death and all of it only deceives you in the few years of your life.

Will you persist in holding on to that which is quickly abandoning you or will you repent of your sins and believe in the God of Abraham, Isaac, Jacob, and Jehoshaphat, even Jesus Christ who came into the world to save sinners?

66

The Hope of the Christian

But Jehoshaphat said, "Is there no prophet of the LORD here, that we may inquire of the LORD by him?" So one of the servants of the king of Israel answered and said, "Elisha the son of Shaphat is here, who poured water on the hands of Elijah."

II Kings 3:11 NKJV

There is a famous story from winter of 1944. As Patton's army was completing one of the greatest military victories in modern history, heavy rain slowed his Third Army's advance. Patton ordered his chaplain to write a prayer for every one of the 250,000 soldiers and civilian personnel attached to the army to pray. The prayer began, *"Almighty and most merciful Father, we humbly beseech Thee, of Thy great goodness to restrain these immoderate rains with which we have had to contend..."* The next day the rain stopped and the Third Army moved north, eventually relieving the 101st Airborne surrounded at Bastogne and turning the Battle of the Bulge from a threatened German revival to a massive Allied victory. For his prayer, Patton awarded his chaplain the Bronze Star.

Patton's moral shortcomings aside (and there were many), in his hour of need in war, Patton in faith or superstitious hope (I do not know which) turned to the Lord, who granted the request of some 250,000 praying soldiers.

Jehoram, the leader of the allies, the supporter of the grand strategy to destroy Moab from the south, was given over to fear and hopelessness, preparing even to be destroyed. But he was not the only king in the wilderness of Edom that day. Jehoshaphat was also there and had a different response to Jehoram's despair: "Is there no prophet of the LORD here, that we may inquire of the Lord...?"

What faith in the hour of need! It reminds us of the same request before the battle with Syria that cost Ahab his life.[1] When times were tough, Jehoshaphat, for all his shortcomings, went to his only hope for help - the Lord God Almighty!

The Lord had delivered Jehoshaphat from the 32 captains of Syria who mistook him for their target Ahab in battle. The Lord had delivered Jehoshaphat when three nations mightier than Judah aligned themselves against him. The Lord was faithful then and Jehoshaphat believed the Lord would be faithful again - and how faithful would the Lord be?

There was a prophet, Elisha the son of Shaphat! He was not just any of the prophets - this was he who served Elijah and succeeded him on his ascension into Heaven. That same Elisha was with them in the wilderness.

If you are trusting in the Lord God of Jehoshaphat today, you are trusting in Jesus Christ who delivers His people from harm. He sets the prisoner free. He takes those in captivity to sin and makes them captives to righteousness and truth, which alone set free. He paid for your sin. He gave you His righteousness. He presents you to the Father. He is sanctifying you even now. And one day soon, He will bring you to glory where you will be in His presence until He returns with glory to judge the world. The hope of the Christian is in the Lord, and the Lord will never cause His people to be ashamed of that properly placed hope!

---

[1] See Devotional 34

67

Elisha Is Here!

But Jehoshaphat said, " Is there no prophet of the LORD here, that we may inquire of the LORD by him?" So one of the servants of the king of Israel answered and said, "Elisha the son of Shaphat is here, who poured water on the hands of Elijah." And Jehoshaphat said, "The word of the LORD is with him." So the king of Israel and Jehoshaphat and the king of Edom went down to him.

II Kings 3:11-12 NKJV

A lot has happened since the last time I was in my Atlanta office in March 2020. The stock market dropped 30% and climbed 40%, only to drop another 8%. More than 20,000,000 Americans lost their jobs. Riots have taken place in cities across America. The political landscape has changed dramatically. More than 120,000 Americans have died from a mysterious disease for which there is no vaccine. The world is bowing down to the idols of critical race theory, bodily autonomy, and ethic gnosticism. Honestly, it is sometimes tempting to sell the house, liquidate the retirement account, pack everything into a truck, and escape with my family to the remote mountains of Montana where I could hike, climb, and mountain bike to my heart's content or at least my last run in with a grizzly. So rapid are the changes around us it can be tempting to try to escape it all.

Do you ever wonder what men like Elisha, Paul, Jeremiah, James, Knox, or Calvin would say if they could see our time? I wonder if they would look around and say, "Nothing new after all this time, men are up to the same wickedness and are still in desperate need of a Savior. What are you and the church doing to proclaim the gospel of repentance and faith in Jesus Christ?"

In this section of II Kings, the questionable alliance of nations had been on the march from Israel for seven days. In the hot wilderness of Edom, with no food or water, the conquerors were in danger of being conquered without even a battle. Surely the Lord's prophets would enjoy the peace and solitude in Samaria for a change now that the king and his army were departed on such a venture. But Elisha was not enjoying the peace in Samaria. Elisha went with the soldiers of Israel and Judah.

Did this allied army seek God before its departure? Not that we are told in Scripture. Did they ask Elisha to come with them? Not that we know of. And yet, following the army or perhaps with the army, was the minister of the Lord of Sabaoth![1]

What joy must have been in the hearts of Jehoshaphat and the fellow believers from the north and the south when they learned the Lord had not abandoned them in the wilderness but had sent His prophet Elisha? In their hour of need, God's minister was with the army. He had endured the hardships of the recent days. He was now ready to serve.

God's servant was where he was needed, which was with the starving armies of Edom, Israel, and Judah. Where are you and I during these distressing times? Are we hiding from the seeming madness around us or will we be ready to give the good tidings of great joy to a lost and dying world? Today, many people want those good tidings to be, "Peace, peace," when there is no peace. They want to hear, "Health is coming, do not fear," when death and misery are on the doorstep. They want to hear of other people searching themselves for and confessing worldly faults publicly, but they do not want to hear the Lord's law and perfect way of righteousness.

---

[1] More to come on this title for the Lord in devotional 70. For now let us understand that this title speaks to the Lord being the leader of all the armies in Heaven and Earth. A blessing to the people of the Lord, a pending disaster to the enemies of the Lord.

What the world needs is the truth. How will the world hear this truth if Christian men and women are hiding from the world? How will the world hear the truth if ministers of the word are not proclaiming the whole counsel of God? The world needs Christians to shine the bright light of Christ in the midst of all the darkness around and from whatever place the Lord has called them. The world needs ministers preaching not about social justice[2] but of the just and holy God who will not let the guilty go free but offers salvation from sin today through Jesus Christ His Son. Perhaps as we live for Christ in the present hour of need, a lost soul will look for a Christian and someone will say, "You are here!"

---

[2] If you need an adjective in front of "justice" there is a high probability that its not the justice spoken of in the Bible. Social justice is the justice society desires at present. In Ancient Rome that meant feeding Christians and other undesirables to the lions. Today that social justice calls you to blaspheme God by cursing or at least lamenting his providence in your birth. Tomorrow it will mean something else.

68

Go to Your Own Prophets!

Then Elisha said to the king of Israel, "What have I to do with you?
Go to the prophets of your father and the prophets of your
mother." But the king of Israel said to him, "No, for the LORD has
called these three kings together to deliver them into the hand of
Moab."

II Kings 3:13 NKJV

My family and I recently watched the movie Amazing Grace,[1] which follows the historical account of William Wilberforce's fight in the British Parliament to end the slave trade and features several highly successful actors. While Wilberforce became a Christian in the early years of adulthood, his friend and eventual prime minister of England, William Pitt (the younger), did not. The movie portrays Pitt as a confident statesman all his life but on his death bed, Pitt is scared and sorrowful, wishing he had the faith of Wilberforce. Hollywood manages to give a poignant example of the fate of all apart from Christ. Regardless of position, power, or wealth, the hour of death comes upon all, for all have sinned and fallen short of the glory of God. For the Christian, the moment of death brings peace to the soul, for it is the entrance into the presence of his Savior. For the unbeliever, it brings fear, for it is the entrance into terrible torment for all eternity.

---

[1] Amazing Grace does not follow the present narrative of revenge, anarchy, and mob rule but rather promotes the truth of God's Word that all men and women regardless of nation, language, or skin color are made in the image of God and equal in His eyes as image bearers. If equal in value in God's eyes, what about our eyes?

Jehoram thought the hour of his death was near and, like Pitt, he was in great fear, for he did not have faith in Jesus Christ. He did not hate and forsake his sin and rest in Christ alone for salvation but was fatalistic and fearful. Even though the Lord showed Jehoram, Jehoshaphat, and the king of Edom great kindness in the presence of Elisha with the armies, still Jehoram had no hope and saw the Lord only coming to destroy him, "for the Lord has called these three kings together to deliver them into the hand of Moab."

Elisha and Elijah had been preaching to Israel and Ahab's family for years only to be threatened, pursued, and mocked. Though its idols had never offered help, Israel was still wholly given over to idolatry. So when Elisha saw Jehoram, he called out the foolish inconsistency. "What do I have to do with you, Jehoram? Go to the prophets of your parents, go to your false gods, let them help you."

Elisha was presenting to Jehoram the greatest punishment of the Lord: giving over the wicked to their wickedness.[2] There would be no help coming from the worthless idols of wood and stone, but God had been telling Israel this for generations. Elisha now, under the inspiration of the Lord, told Jehoram to go to those idols. Plead with them for help. This giving over was to show Jehoram and us the utter worthlessness of the false gods of the day. They cannot help us.[3]

When the day of death comes upon you (and it will, for it is appointed once for men to die, then afterwards the judgment Heb. 9:27), will you be looking to the Word of the Lord for help or to the LGBTQ+ and allies community to give you comfort? Will bodily autonomy sustain you through the valley of the shadow of death that you did not autonomously choose to walk through? You do not need to wait to find that the answer is no. But there is

---

[2] Romans 1:24,26,28.

[3] See Isaiah 46:1-7.

a remedy for such hopelessness: it is the Lord of Elisha, Jesus Christ Himself. He says, *"Ho, everyone who thirsts, come to the waters; and you who have no money, come, buy, and eat. Yes, come, buy wine and milk without money and without price. Why do you spend money for what is not bread, and your wages for what does not satisfy? Listen carefully to Me, and eat what is good, and let your soul delight itself in abundance. Incline your ear, and come to Me. Hear, and your soul shall live... Seek the LORD while He may be found, call upon Him while He is near. Let the wicked forsake his way, and the unrighteousness man his thoughts; Let him return to the LORD, and He will have mercy on him; and to our God, for He will abundantly pardon"* (Isaiah 55:1-7 NKJV).

Do not go to your deathbed in fear and agony like Jehoram and Pitt, but go with hope and rejoicing that the LORD is with you.

69

What If There Is One Righteous?

And Elisha said, " As the LORD of hosts lives, before whom I stand, surely were it not that I regard the presence of Jehoshaphat king of Judah, I would not look at you, nor see you. But now bring me a musician." Then it happened, when the musician played, that the hand of the LORD came upon him.

II Kings 3:14-15 NKJV

When Sodom's sin had reached the point where the Lord was going to destroy it, Abraham prayed to God that He might spare the city if the Lord found ten righteous in it. The Lord promised Abraham that if there were ten righteous in the whole city of Sodom He would not destroy the city.[1] When Elisha spoke to the three kings in vs. 14, he said it was because of one righteous man in their presence that he was even willing to look at the group and deliver the Word of God.

We should not take Elisha's words against Jehoram as mere insult but rather as the mind of the Lord against wicked Jehoram. It was not because of Jehoram that the Lord would speak but rather because of godly Jehoshaphat. The sense is that without righteous Jehoshaphat there in the wilderness that day, the armies would have been given up to thirst, hunger, and defeat at the hands of the Moabites. But because of the mercy of the Lord, one righteous man was sufficient for the Lord to deal graciously with the whole host. Even if Jehoshaphat sinned in joining with Edom and Israel in this war, yet the Lord would use it for the saving of many lives in that wilderness.

---

[1] Genesis 19:32

In Abraham's day God would have relented for 10 righteous in Sodom, but they were not found. In Elisha's day, the Lord preserved the allies for just one righteous man. In Ezekiel's day, the Lord looked at the terrible sins of Israel and searched again for one righteous man, but He found none.[2]

We know from Scripture there are no men who are righteous of their own merit. Jehoshaphat's righteousness was not his own but had been given to him by another, for there is none righteous, no, not one.[3] All have sinned and fallen short of the glory of God. Who then will make a wall and stand in the gap for you and for me that the wrath and fire of God might not be poured out against us for our unrighteousness?

Since there were none righteous, the Lord promised through Jeremiah the prophet that the days were coming when the Lord would raise unto David a righteous Branch, and a King (Jer. 23:5). God Himself would send the Righteous One to stand in the gap for His people, to make atonement for the sins of many, and to make righteous by imputing His righteousness on them (II Cor. 5:21). This righteous Branch that was coming has by God's marvelous grace now come. His name is "Jesus Christ the righteous" (I John 2:1).

Jehoshaphat was not the hope of the world. He was righteous because God had made Him righteous. But as Jehoshaphat was in that wilderness with those kings, the Lord regarded Jehoshaphat to teach us this valuable lesson today. If the Lord spared the army of three nations because of the presence of Jehoshaphat, how much more will He save to all eternity His elect children who have

---

[2] "So I sought for a man among them who would make a wall, and stand in the gap before Me on behalf of the land, that I should not destroy it; but I found no one. Therefore I have poured out My indignation on them; I have consumed them with the fire of My wrath; and I have recompensed their deeds on their own heads," says the Lord God" (Ezekiel 22:30-31).

[3] Romans 3:10-12

been washed with the blood of the one righteous man, Jesus Christ?

When Jesus was taken to the cross of Calvary, a far greater battle had been raging. All mankind by their fall had lost communion with God, were under His wrath and curse, and were made liable to His just punishment and to Hell itself.[4] But one righteous man, the God Man, Jesus Christ, stood in the gap for His elect people and paid the just penalty for our sins to the Father. He died on that cross and rose again on the third day. So all who repent of their sins and believe in Jesus Christ for salvation are no longer enemies of the Father, but beloved children. The warfare is ended. The iniquity is pardoned. Is the Righteous one your God today?[5]

---

[4] See Westminster Shorter Catechism Q&A #19

[5] I limited my comments on verse 15. The Lord works in many different ways to bring His Word through the prophets to the intended audience. He can use fire from Heaven; a staff that turns into a serpent, or even music as He does here. We should note that the divinely inspired Psalms were specifically written for use with musical accompaniment and we still sing them to the present day.

70

The Lord of Sabaoth: His Promise

And he said, "Thus says the LORD: 'Make this valley full of ditches.'
For thus says the LORD: 'You shall not see wind, nor shall you see
rain; yet that valley shall be filled with water, so that you, your
cattle, and your animals may drink.' And this is a simple matter in
the sight of the LORD; He will also deliver the Moabites into your
hand. Also you shall attack every fortified city and every choice
city, and shall cut down every good tree, and stop up every spring
of water, and ruin every good piece of land with stones."

II Kings 3:16-19 NKJV

Twice in the English Bible we read the name of the Lord as the "Lord of Sabaoth." The first instance is in Romans 9:29 where we read, "And as Isaiah said before: Unless the Lord of Sabaoth had left us a seed, we would have become like Sodom, and we would have been made like Gomorrah." If you then search Isaiah for this quotation, you wont have to go far: in Isaiah 1:9 we find this quotations which begins, "Unless the Lord of hosts..." The Greek word translated Sabaoth in English is derived from the Hebrew word translated more than 200 times in the OT as "Hosts".

The title refers to the Lord being the "self-existing One," the "One who is," "I Am," Jehovah; and leader of the armies and angels of Heaven, the hosts. It is the Lord of Sabaoth who is with us in Psalm 46:7. It is a title specifically applied to Jesus, the Redeemer, throughout Isaiah[1] and to the one who divided the seas. It is a title and description of the LORD that demonstrates great power, both over the armies of heaven and also over every living creature.

---

[1] See Isaiah 44:6, Isaiah 47:4, Isaiah 54:5

Even the winds and the waves obey the voice of the Lord of Sabaoth.

Elisha had reminded the kings of the greatness of the Lord by using the title, the Lord of Hosts, for the name of God whom Elisha served (vs.14). While the music was playing in the wilderness of Edom, the Lord of Sabaoth made his promise known. Two great events would take place: 1) water would be provided in abundance for all living creatures in the army to drink (vs. 17); and Moab would be utterly decimated (vs. 19).

First, the Lord would show forth His provision. The immediate need was nourishment for the body, and God was going to provide water in a miraculous way. The armies would dig trenches and ditches which would fill with water without wind or rain. Enough water would come to quench the thirst of every man and beast. The water would also be clean and not polluted or dirty as would be the case if the water simply made its way in a flash flood from heavy rains many miles away in Edom. This would be good water from the Lord, the giver of Living Water.

The promised provision was a remarkable display of the Lord's power over creation. He ordained water to come from Edom without anybody feeling wind or seeing rain. And what is great and miraculous to man is a very simple matter in the sight of the Lord (vs. 18). We must ask our God for hard things, for what is difficult for man is simple for God. Cannot God do hard things today?

Secondly, the Lord would give the alliance more than they could ask or think. He would not simply provide for their physical nourishment in the wilderness; He would enable them to utterly destroy Moab. The Moabites would be delivered into their hand (vs 18). The destruction promised was calamity and disaster upon Moab. Water stopped, cities pulled apart stone by stone, crops destroyed, and land ruined. The destruction Jehoram feared was coming upon the allies would be poured out upon Moab tenfold because the Lord of Hosts would fight for this army.

All of our daily bread and protection comes from the Lord of Sabaoth. May we be still and know that the Lord is God. For "the Lord of Hosts is with us; the God of Jacob is our refuge" (Psalm 46:7;11).

71

The Lord Sends Water

"Now it happened in the morning, when the grain offering was offered, that suddenly water came by way of Edom, and the land was filled with water."

II Kings 3:20 NKJV

D o you remember what time of day it was when God sent fire down from heaven to consume the sacrifice on the top of Mt. Carmel in the sight of all Israel? I Kings 18:36 tells us it was at the time of the evening sacrifice. In the Old Testament church, there were two primary times of sacrifices of worship to the Lord, the morning sacrifice and the evening sacrifice. Certain things were done at each. This pattern is often used as part of the basis for morning and evening worship on the Lord's Day.

It seems that several of the Lord's great wonders in the days of Elijah and Elisha were meant to be timed to remind those present and the readers today of the worship of God alone. The great works of the Lord are given that we might know who God is, how great and powerful is His might, His ability to save to the uttermost, and our only response must be thanksgiving and worship before His throne.

The Lord sent fire from Heaven at the time of the evening sacrifice on Mt. Carmel for all Israel to see. The Lord sent water to fill the wilderness at the time of the morning sacrifice and in the sight of the armies from three nations. This should have been an hour of prayer for all gathered and certainly was for the godly among the allied camp. It was at this hour when half of the flour for a grain offering was to be offered before the Lord in worship (Leviticus

6:20). At this solemn time, the Lord sent water by the way of Edom and the land was filled with water such that every man and beast was able to drink their fill. Surely this should remind us of our need for the Living Water from the Lord.

Some might argue that the water came by natural occurrence, "by way of Edom" such as we might see in a flash flood many miles away and a river appearing without a cloud in the sky. I do not want to deny that the Lord can and does use His providence in and through nature to bring about His promises. He certainly could have done this here. Nevertheless, the description in verse 17 suggests something taking place at least partially above nature. The army was very large, encamped over a large space, and no one saw rain or heard wind. Flash floods do not find ditches to fill and stop or move on to other ditches. They carve rivers in deserts and destroy all in their path. The water is filthy from dirt and debris picked up on the way and anyone caught in the path of a major flood would be drowned. The water by the way of Edom filled the ditches in the valley that the army dug apparently without any harm to man or beast.

Let us learn from this portion of God's Holy Word these two things: 1) To pray and worship God when we rise up in the morning and before we go to sleep in the evening (and throughout the day in between); and 2) As the Lord promises, so He always does.

"Remember the former things of old, for I am God, and there is none else; I am God and there is none like me, declaring the end from the beginning, and form ancient times the things that are not yet done, saying, "My counsel shall stand, and I will do all My pleasure" (Isaiah 46:9-10).

72

The Lord Fools the Moabites

And when all the Moabites heard that the kings had come up to fight against them, all who were able to bear arms and older were gathered; and they stood at the border. Then they rose up early in the morning, and the sun was shining on the water; and the Moabites saw the water on the other side as red as blood. And they said, "This is blood; the kings have surely struck swords and have killed one another; now therefore, Moab, to the spoil!"

II Kings 3:21-23 NKJV

There are some portions of Scripture on which godly men take polar opposite views. The account of Rahab and the spies in Joshua chapter 2 is one such account. Many men have claimed Rahab's misleading (might we even say deceiving?) the soldiers of Jericho who came to her door was a great sin. Others, looking to Hebrews 11:31 and James 2:25 claim that hiding the spies and deceiving the soldiers was the very act of faith for which the Lord praised Rahab through all generations. It seems to me evident from the Lord's work at Jericho, Ai a few chapters later, Gideon and the 300, Ehud and Eglon, and many other places that deceit in war is a providential gift of God. It does not open the door for breaking the 9th commandment but rather teaches us that the 9th commandment was never intended to forbid deceit as a strategy of war for the saving of many lives.

Our text today provides another example of the Lord using His great works to trick the enemies of His people. The same water that miraculously came into the wilderness of Edom and saved the three armies was then used by God to deceive the Moabites.

Word had spread that Israel, Judah, and Edom were coming against Moab's southern border and were suffering from exhaustion. The Moabites gathered every soldier and older man that could bear arms and went to the border to prepare for the battle. When they woke up in the morning the water they saw in the distance appeared to them to be pools and rivers of blood. Why would they make such an interpretation of the water?

We must remember two things. First, in II Chronicles 20, a few years before this event, the Moabites, Ammonites, and Mt. Seir went up to attack Jehoshaphat and Jerusalem. Instead of destroying Judah, however, the Lord caused the three armies to fight each other so that when Judah arrived on the battlefield, all the soldiers of the enemy armies were dead and Judah had nothing to do but carry away the spoil. Second, Judah, Israel, and Edom were known not to have been friends. They had fought with each other many times. The idea of these allies suddenly becoming enemies in the wilderness of Edom was easy for the Moabites to believe, especially when the same thing had happened to Moab just a few years prior.

For these reasons, when the Lord caused the Moabites to see the water as blood, they were convinced that the allies had turned on one another and a great victory was on the Moabites' doorstep: "Moab, to the spoil!"

Those great works and miracles of the Lord that are used to the saving of many can often be used to the destruction of the enemies of the Lord. Many saw Lazarus raised from the dead in John 11 and went away to tell the Pharisees. The miracle of Christ that led to salvation for some and increase of faith for others also led to greater condemnation of the unbelievers present. They saw Christ, the Resurrection and the Life, and they rejected Him. The Lord used His great work in the wilderness of Edom to lead the Moabites to utter ruin. May we trust the Lord whose works are very great and tell of these works to the generation following.

73

God's Judgment on Moab

So when they came to the camp of Israel, Israel rose up and attacked the Moabites, so that they fled before them; and they entered their land, killing the Moabites. Then they destroyed the cities, and each man threw a stone on every good piece of land and filled it; and they stopped up all the springs of water and cut down all the good trees. But they left the stones of Kir-Haraseth intact. However, the slingers surrounded and attacked it.

II Kings 3:24-25 NKJV

God's judgment on the wicked continues to be a less than pleasant topic in most places today. Some Christian churches seem to outrightly ignore it because it does not produce the good feelings they are so hungry to generate. "But the wrath of God is revealed from heaven against all ungodliness and unrighteousness of men, who suppress the truth in unrighteousness..." (Rom. 1:18).

Remember, it was the Lord in verses 19-20 who told the allies to attack every fortified city, every choice city, to cut down every good tree, to stop up every spring of water, and ruin every good piece of land with stones. It wasn't Jehoram's plan for all we know he just wanted his lamb and wool tributes back. God called for the destruction of the whole country.

First, the destruction of the army took place. Have you ever been looking forward to a great event taking place only to see the opposite actually happen? I have seen this on a few occasions and it is demoralizing. The Moabite army expected to be looting and pillaging by lunch. Instead, they found a very much alive army that rose up and attacked, causing them to rapidly retreat.

Next they ravaged the land. The idea here was not merely military defeat but an utter destruction and humiliation of the whole of Moab. The rock walls were torn down and thrown into the farmers' fields so that the cities were left undefended and the ground was left unusable for farming.

Finally, they stopped up the springs or wells of water so that water would be unavailable to drink and they cut down the trees so that they could neither eat their fruit nor build homes and cities from their wood. The judgment of God was great and terrible. Only one fortified city was left intact, the fortress Kir Haraseth, and this is where the king of Moab and his remaining soldiers fled for safety. The allies quickly besieged this city and the slingers attacked it.

We must not fool ourselves into thinking God's wrath will not be poured out on all unrighteousness. To promote and believe the full counsel of God includes promoting and believing in the wrath and judgment of God. The Lord has judged in the past, is judging in the present, and Jesus even refers to the day of His future return as Judgment Day. [1] Do not fear the wicked, this day of judgment is coming. Do not be wicked, the day of judgment is coming. Escape the wrath of God on that day of judgment, trust in Jesus Christ and repent of your sins.[2]

---

[1] Matthew 12:36, Mark 6:11, I John 4:17; Jude 6; 2 Peter 2:9, 3:7.

[2] See Westminster Shorter Catechism Q&A #85.

74

The Breakout Attempt

And when the king of Moab saw that the battle was too fierce for him, he took with him seven hundred men who drew swords, to break through to the king of Edom, but they could not.

II Kings 3:26 NKJV

In late 1942, the battle of Stalingrad had been engaged for many months. The Russian winter had led the Red Army to realize not only that the battle for Stalingrad could be won but that a great Russian victory could be achieved over the German 6th Army. The key to Russian victory was to attack the southern flanks of the German army, which were made up of weak Romanian troops. By the end of the first day's offensive, the 3rd and 4th Romanian armies were in headlong retreat. Three days later, Red Army forces from the north met with Red Army forces from the south and the 6th German Army was surrounded in Stalingrad where it would be destroyed.

The king of Moab was surrounded, his nation was destroyed, and while he did not hope for a victory at Kir-Haraseth, he was hoping to survive. His plan was similar to that of the Russians many years later: Attack the weakest link in the enemy line. That was the army of the king of Edom. Israel and Judah had aligned themselves for the battle and developed the plan, and the king of Edom seemed to have joined towards the end of the plan and provided access through his wilderness to attack Moab. Perhaps, after already participating in a great victory, his troops would retreat with a sudden and severe breakthrough attempt by the king of Moab.

The plight of Moab at this stages was such that this daring attempt with a measure of wisdom behind it was still doomed to failure. The 700 choice men remaining from Moab were unable to break through the encirclement and escape to fight another day.

When a nation is destroyed, peace would seem to be the logical pursuit but that was not the case with Moab. The king wanted to escape rather than admit defeat and submit himself again to the kings surrounding Moab.

The Lord's blocking this escape was for at least two reasons: 1) The Lord had promised to destroy Moab, and if the king had escaped in a last strategic hurrah, Moab would achieve a small strategic victory in the end; and 2) The Lord allowed one more deed to reveal the great heights of evil that Moab and surrounding nations had achieved.

When our sins destroy us it seems logical to pursue peace with God. Peace is freely offered through Jesus Christ, the Prince of Peace, but many will rally their strength to break away from the Lord or commit even greater evil rather than submit themselves to Him. Let us pray for ourselves and the others to submit wholly to the Lord and King Jesus Christ.

75

The Depravity of Moab: The Sacrifice

Then he took his eldest son who would have reigned in his place, and offered him as a burnt offering upon the wall; and there was great indignation against Israel. So they departed from him and returned to their own land.

II Kings 3:27 NKJV

When visiting the Answers in Genesis's Ark Encounter last year, one area had a display of some of the many popular characterizations of Noah's Ark available for the consumer. This included stuffed animals, coloring books, and every imaginable children's book on the flood. Nearly all of the items in the display showed fun fairy-tale-like representations of what was the most violent, deadly event in human history. The exhibit was expressing how these types of children's books and toys unintentionally undermine the seriousness of the flood by making it seem like something fun and childish in contrast to something deadly and fearful. The flood account should be told with less emphasis on cuddly giraffes and more on the judgment of God on the wicked and the mercy of God on His children.

The Scripture is ripe with violent accounts of God's judgment and sin to leave us without excuse or ignorance as to the wages and consequences of sin. These accounts turn many people away from God's Word or cause what was violent to be ameliorated. If we abandon the Word or distort the Bible over these hard accounts we would be turning our backs on the truth. The way of man's sin leads only to cruelty, misery, and death itself. This reality is on display throughout Scripture but rarely as shockingly as the last verse of II Kings 3.

The end of the allies' campaign into Moab was as abrupt as it was violent. Something took place that I have never seen recorded in a children's Bible story book or painted as a mural in a nursery. The king of Moab, having just failed to break out of Kir-Haraseth, decided that the desperate time called for terrible measures. He took his oldest son, the heir to the throne of Moab, the strength of his youth, a prince, and killed him publicly on the wall of the city for all the Israelites, Edomites, and Moabites to see. We don't know the son's age, but his blood was shed by his own father on the wall to somehow appease Chemosh, the demonic idol and abomination of Moab, and to startle the invaders into ending their conquest at that time.

Matthew Henry says in his commentary on this chapter, "The dearer any thing was to them the more acceptable those idolaters thought it must needs be if offered in sacrifice to their gods, and therefore burnt their children in the fire to their honor." The demonic idols of this world require blood, and so the world gives them blood.

When the Moabites saw the terrible end their king was driven to because of the siege, there was great anger against Israel, and Israel in turn lifted the siege and everyone returned to their own countries.

I remember reading that towards the end of the battle of Okinawa, Japanese mothers, having been told lies about the barbarity of the Americans to captured children, began throwing their children off of cliffs so that they would die in less cruel manners than they feared. Many of the mothers then threw themselves from the cliffs. The Americans pulled back their soldiers and sent in Japanese translators with megaphones to plead with the people not to kill themselves or their children. I have wondered if perhaps Israel withdrew for a similar reason, so that the Moabites would not offer more of their children as human sacrifices and that future generations might hear of the wickedness of Moab laid bare: The king killed his son for a burnt sacrifice on the wall.

Let us not shy away from the violent portions of Scripture or twist them into something fun, but let us teach them truthfully and soberly. It is very likely that the same evil of thousands of years ago is taking place now, and it is certain the judgment of God, like in the days of Noah, is coming again. Oh that men would turn to the Lord in faith in this great hour of need!

76

Abominations in Moab, Abominations in America

Then he took his eldest son who would have reigned in his place, and offered him as a burnt offering upon the wall; and there was great indignation against Israel. So they departed from him and returned to their own land.

II Kings 3:27 NKJV

Recent months are manifesting a particular perspective on history. The past is filled with evil characters, twisted thinking, abuse, and sin, while the present is filled with good people, proper thinking, and justice seekers. Those promoting this perspective encourage us to appraise their movements. They advocate "social justice," tear down statues of anyone with questionable associations, and promote the lives of those they deem marginalized and abused. They view today's generation as superior to past generations, for we have evolved into more enlightened human beings.

There is just one problem with this perspective. Our generation is committing violence every day on a scale that I suspect most characters in history would find startling. The king of Moab offered his son as a burnt sacrifice on a wall in front of many; in our day, millions of people offer their unborn and partially born sons and daughters to the same demons in the rooms of Planned Parenthood and abortion "clinics" around the country. One would think that nearly one million murders per year of the most vulnerable would be sufficient to gain the top spot in the world rankings of child murder, but it isn't. The blood of innocent children has washed over many lands for so long and so completely that many have stopped noticing. Very few are angry at the child offerings being made to the abominations of our land, such as bodily autonomy and the deadly philosophy of "a woman's right to choose" to murder the life within her womb.

If the horror of the king's sacrifice was sufficient for Israel to end their military campaign into Moab, what response should the horror of today's parents shedding the blood of their children all over our land elicit from us? This one verse from II Kings 3 can remind us to do several things:

First, pray for the Lord to end the shedding of innocent blood. Unless the Lord of Sabaoth intervenes, we can have little hope of seeing an end to the wickedness swiftly approaching its 50th year of legalization. "Can a mother forget the baby at her breast and have no compassion on the child she has borne? Though she may forget, I will not forget you" (Isaiah 49:15). Pray for the Lord to remember the cry of innocent blood and to intervene and save from the slaughter.

Second, be a faithful witness of the Word of the Lord to a lost and dying world. The topic of murder is coming up regularly in conversation these days as the world focuses on the taking of innocent life. Christians can testify to the biblical reasons to hate murder, such as all people being made in the image of God (Gen. 1:27); the Lord specifically forbidding murder (Ex. 20:13); and the Lord hating murder (Prov. 6:16-19). Then the Christian can direct the conversation to the most widespread murder in all the world and the only murder that is widely celebrated and give witness to the life in the womb. "Before I formed you in the womb I knew you, before you were born I set you apart" (Jeremiah 1:5). "From birth I was cast on you; from my mother's womb you have been my God" (Psalm 22:10).

Third, in your various places, relations, and callings, be a defender of innocent life. God has put us all in different places, with different gifts and abilities. Within those various places, we will have opportunities to take a stand for life. For some people that may be witnessing outside of Planned Parenthood. For others that may counseling pregnant women who are worried about financial and social costs and considering abortion. For others it may be counseling boyfriends and parents who are ashamed of a girlfriend or daughter who is pregnant and unable to care for the child on her own. These situations are very common and the Lord may put you in these people's lives to be a witness to them of the blessing of life in the womb, hope in all circumstances through Jesus Christ our Lord, and forgiveness of all sins through His death on the cross and resurrection the third day.

What if through the prayers of the saints, the witness of Christians, and the assistance we give in the places the Lord has put us God would cause the world to see the abomination that abortion is and bring it swiftly to an end even as He has ended great evils in the past.

If this were published only for Bible-believing Christians we might stop here, but I hope those who are not Christians might also read this, perhaps those considering an abortion, perhaps those who have already had abortions in the past. It can be difficult to read about one's own sin. While I have not been involved in an abortion, my sins are many and I read of them nearly every day in the Scripture along with the promised curse for my sin, even death and eternal hell-fire. Why then should you or I care about our sin, abortion, or anything else? What hope is there? Why even read this?

The Lord who is rich in grace and abundant in mercy sent His only Son Jesus Christ to die to bear the wrath and curse of God in our place so that we might not die but have everlasting life. For whom did He die? Whoever believes in Him (John 3:16). Whoever confesses their sins, He promises to forgive (I John 1:9). The sin of abortion is in God's power to forgive. God can turn your mourning into gladness. If you will today confess your sins to the Lord and believe in Him alone for salvation, you will be forgiven and have eternal life.

"Have mercy upon me, O God, according to Your lovingkindness; according to the multitude of Your tender mercies, blot out my transgressions. Wash me thoroughly from my iniquity, and cleanse me from my sin... Hide Your face from my sins, and blot out all my iniquities. Create in me a clean heart, O God, and renew a steadfast spirit within me" Psalm 51:1-2,9-10.

77

The Widow's Plight

A certain woman of the wives of the sons of the prophets cried out to Elisha, saying, "Your servant my husband is dead, and you know that your servant feared the LORD. And the creditor is coming to take my two sons to be his slaves."

II Kings 4:1 NKJV

D o you regard widows the way God regards widows in the Bible? When is the last time you considered your own heart towards the widows around you in church and among your neighbors?

God provides particularly special care in Scripture for those people who by reason of God's providence are most vulnerable to harm or mistreatment. There are typically three categories, the sojourner (stranger, foreigner, or alien), the fatherless child, and the widow. "You shall not mistreat a stranger nor oppress him, for you were stranger in the land of Egypt. You shall not afflict any widow or fatherless child. If you afflict them in any way, and they cry at all to Me, I will surely hear their cry; and My wrath will become hot, and I will kill you with the sword; your wives shall be widows, and your children fatherless" (Exodus 22:21-24).

Just after the giving of the Ten Commandments, God said, "You shall not afflict any widow, or fatherless child" (Ex. 20:22). When the blessings and the curses were read routinely in Israel, all the people would hear, "Cursed be he that perverted the judgment of the stranger, fatherless, and widow. And all the people shall say, Amen" (Deut. 27:19). When the widow put two mites into the temple treasury, Jesus commended the woman who gave of her want unto the Lord (Mark 12:41-44). Jesus raised the widows only son at Nain (Luke 7:11-17). The care for widows was a part of the ministries of Elijah, Jesus, and Elisha as we will now see.

As we come to II Kings 4, we find that Elisha was back in Israel with the sons of the prophets, and one of the men had died.[1] This prophet left behind a wife who was then a widow, two sons, some financial debt, and this legacy: He was a servant of Elisha and feared the Lord (vs. 1).[2]

The financial debt was the immediate problem. The creditor was coming to make good the payment by taking the two sons of the widow to be his slaves. This was a serious problem for at least two reasons: 1) It was afflicting both the widow and the fatherless; and 2) Though a creditor could require a debtor to work for him to pay off the debt, he must be treated as a hired servant (employee) and could not serve as a bond servant or slave. Furthermore, he was to be set free in the year of Jubilee (Lev. 25:39-40). It seems evident from this account that there was great injustice. Rather than debts being cancelled with the death of the man, the debt was being called by creating greater hardship on the fatherless children and their widowed mother.

---

[1] The timing of chapter 4 is not perfectly clear. Certainly there are portions of II Kings that are not in chronological order, but the Lord is highlighting several of the miracles Elisha performed by God's power that established him as the prophet of the Lord with a double portion of Elijah's spirit. It is possible this event took place after Elisha returned from Moab. It is also possible that it took place between chapters 2 and 3.

[2] We ought to give regular thought to our legacy in this fashion: How will we be remembered by our families in relationship to the Lord? Will our families even think of us in relation to the Lord? Or will they think of our love for the world, beer, parties, football, hiking, or movies above all else? We know nothing of this prophet who died other than he left behind a believing wife, obedient sons, and this testimony: "He feared the Lord." There are few better eulogies or tombstone inscriptions that could be made than this.

What injustice and misery was in Israel that the widow could not go to the local governor but had to plead with Elisha the prophet for help! When the true God is denied and idols are served in His place, all manner of injustice and sin will prevail. We have the stranger, fatherless, and widow with us today. May we help them in every godly way we can that the name of Christ might be exalted in the world when they see us caring for one another's needs. "By this all will know that you are My disciples, if you have love for one another" (John 13:35).

78

Down But Not Out

*So Elisha said to her, "What shall I do for you? Tell me, what do
you have in the house?" And she said, "Your maidservant has
nothing in the house but a jar of oil."*

II Kings 4:2 NKJV

Peter and John went to the temple shortly after the day of
Pentecost and met a man who was more than forty years
old and lame from birth. Each day he was carried to the
Beautiful Gate to ask alms of those going into the temple. Hoping
to receive some money, he looked to Peter and John and Peter
said, "Silver and gold I do not have, but what I do have I give you;
in the name of Jesus Christ of Nazareth, rise up and walk" (Acts
3:1-10). Immediately his feet and ankle bones were restored and
he went walking and leaping into the temple all the while praising
God.

Like that lame man in Jerusalem, so the widow in Israel was
helpless against the impending calamity facing the remainder of
her family.

The widow looked for help from Elisha and presented a sizeable
financial need. Eviction notices and past due utility bills do not
come close to the pressure of having one's two sons taken into
slavery as this woman faced. Surely Elisha would give the woman
money! But he did not. Elisha wanted her faith to be strengthened
through this process and all generations to learn something from
this widow of the salvation of the Lord. Instead of giving money,
Elisha asked the woman two questions: What shall I do for you?
Tell me, what do you have in your house?

The first question seemed to acknowledge the prophets' lack of wealth. They were in hiding for many years, hated and mocked by many of the residents of the towns, so money was difficult to come by. Often times when Christians are persecuted they are forbidden from stable means of income and uses of their God-given talents. Poverty can come quickly even with hard work and without any sin on the individual's part. Debt is a likely acquaintance of such circumstances. This prophet who died feared the Lord, so, likely was not sinfully in debt. Elisha was once a man with considerable means but had given that up for the riches of telling people the word of the Lord. Silver and gold Elisha did not have for the widow: "What shall I do for you?" But, such as Elisha had, the double portion of Elijah's spirit, he would do for her all that the Lord would provide: "Tell me, what do you have in your house?"*

A stranger asked me for a few dollars in cash a few months ago. I told him I did not have any cash but as a Christian I would like to help as I could. I asked about his present condition and he responded that he needed cash, would I help? When I repeated my original request for information he said a few rough words and left. When Elisha asked the faithful widow what she had, she did not turn away in disgust, but out of the abundance of her need, she told of her current material possessions. Inside her house she had nothing but a jar of oil. Everything else seems to have been sold to pay the creditors. Perhaps like the widow of Zarephath she was storing a small amount to make one last meal for her family before they were taken away.

Notice the faith of this woman. Like her husband, she clearly feared the Lord and trusted that in every situation the Lord can and would provide. Though Elisha loved the prophets and their families very much, the events that follow do not testify to Elisha's great benevolence; rather they testify to the mercy and love of the Lord which endures forever for His people.

Friends, the Lord does not always provide in the way we expect. The most the lame man hoped for was some money from Peter and John. Instead, he listened to the apostles and received healing from the Lord in a way he probably had stopped hoping for. When Elisha did not produce money, the widow did not lose hope but maintained her trust in the Lord. Let us not hope in a particular outcome from the Lord but hope in the Lord Himself. He provides far more abundantly than we can imagine or think.

79

Elisha the Deacon

Then he said, "Go, borrow vessels from everywhere, from all your neighbors - empty vessels; do not gather just a few. And when you have come in, you shall shut the door behind you and your sons; then pour it into all those vessels, and set aside the full ones." So she went from him and shut the door behind her and her sons, who brought the vessels to her; and she poured it out. Now it came to pass, when the vessels were full, that she said to her son, "Bring me another vessel." And he said to her, "There is not another vessel."

II Kings 4:3-6 NKJV

The office of deacon is a very difficult office and often under-appreciated in the church. The biblical care of those in need requires discernment and wisdom from the Lord. The challenges that the poor and needy face are difficult to ascertain completely in a short amount of time, and the work is often long-term in nature with few overnight results. But the Lord does not leave deacons without infallible wisdom from God. I Timothy 5 is one of the guiding portions of Scripture for financial diaconal care. It uses the example of widows who are to be the highest priority of the deacons alongside orphans and foreigners. Certainly able-bodied men ought not to be given more than widows.

What is noteworthy about I Timothy 5 is its focus on how not to care for widows. Don't financially support widows with family who can care for her. Don't financially support a widow unless she is at least sixty years old and has a good reputation. Don't financially support widows who can support themselves. Only relieve those widows whose need is great.

The widow in Israel had sold all she owned and she and her two sons were down to one jar of oil. She was desperately poor and had no where else to turn. While the Lord was going to provide for her abundantly by His miraculous work, she had to labor toward the outcome and obey the words of Elisha. He gave her unusual instructions: Go borrow vessels from everywhere, from all your neighbors, as many as you can!

If this account is chronologically after the war with Moab, the instruction might have reminded the widow as it reminds us of God's command to the allies in the wilderness of Edom to "make this valley full of ditches..." (3:16). Do not expect the Lord to do a small work, but make ready for a great work that the Lord will do. After this gathering and preparing the vessels the widow would close the door and pour her oil into each borrowed vessel.

The widow did not ask what the Lord would do from this activity; she trusted the Lord and His prophet. As she poured the oil from her jar into each vessel, the oil was multiplied miraculously by God and never ran out, not even when there were no more vessels to fill.

The Lord has given us yet another exemplary measure of faith displayed in the widows of Scripture. Out of the abundance of their need came an abundance of faith in the Lord who satisfies all our needs. May we learn from this widow in Israel, the widow of Zarephath, and the widow with the two mites to do two things: Trust in the Lord at all times and obey His holy word.

80

The Lord Pays and Provides

Then she came and told the man of God. And he said, "Go, sell the oil and pay your debt; and you and your sons live on the rest."

II Kings 4:7 NKJV

While there are many trials in life we must bear, there are also events in our lives that seem too good to be true. I still look back with amazement on my engagement that my now wife said "yes" to marrying me. I often reflect on the way the Lord has afforded protection to my family even during times of great loss. As I sit here writing, I marvel that the Lord would show such kindness to this wretched sinner for so many years. And what greater mercy in all of life that the Lord not only paid the debt and penalty for my sins but also gave me eternal life. What wondrous love is this?

The widow just witnessed a great miracle of the Lord alone in her home with her two sons. Her one last jar of oil filled countless vessels of oil. That which was of very limited value was used by God to create a quantity of oil of great value. It was such a great miracle that she did not know what to do, so she went back to Elisha to tell him. Elisha instructed her to use this miraculous kindness of God for her own provision: Sell the oil, pay the debt, and live with your sons on the rest of the proceeds.

We were introduced to this widow as she faced a major problem: Her sons would be taken into slavery. The reason for the problem was the debt her family owed. With this overwhelming burden before her, how could she have imagined being released from her debt much less how she could support herself and her children even if her debt were paid. And here is what the Lord did: He gave her an abundance of oil so that the debt might be paid in full. But He also gave her more than enough to pay the debt. He gave her enough to live with her sons without fear of poverty or starvation.

How can we think about this verse without considering the gifts of the Lord in the greatest mercy of all, the sending of His own Son, Jesus Christ, to die on the cross and rise from the dead on the third day? What happened with that greatest of events in history? Jesus Christ paid my debt. Galatians 3:13 says, "Christ has redeemed us from the curse of the law, having become a curse for us (for it is written, 'Cursed is everyone who hangs on a tree...')". "For He hath made Him to be sin for us, who knew no sin..." (II Cor. 5:21).

We must remember, the proceeds from the oil did not only pay the family's debt, and the death and resurrection of Christ did not only pay the debt and curse of my sin. It also gave life! "And I give unto them eternal life; and they shall never perish..." (John 10:28). "These things have I written to you who believe in the name of the Son of God; that you may know that you have eternal life, and that you may continue to believe in the name of the Son of God" (I John 5:13).

When you remember the widow in Israel in the days of Elisha, remember her for her exemplary faith in the Lord; and remember that the Lord not only miraculously provided the payment for her family's debt but also provided for the substance of her family's life. To God be all praise and glory!

81

A Notable Woman from a Notable Town

Now it happened one day that Elisha went to Shunem, where there was a notable woman, and she persuaded him to eat some food. So it was, as often as he passed by, he would turn in there to eat some food.

II Kings 4:8 NKJV

What makes a person great in the annals of history? There is nothing about the names of Alexander the Great, Julius Caesar, Augustine of Hippo, John Calvin, or George Washington that marks their bearers as worthy of renown? Rather, we recognize these names because of the notable acts that these men did in history. If it weren't for their deeds, we would not recognize their names. Because of their deeds, we recognize their names. Consider then the widow of Zarephath; the one leper in ten who returned to the Lord with thanksgiving; the Samaritan woman; and the centurion whose servant was healed.

Consider also the widow at Nain. The day after Jesus healed the centurion's servant in Luke 7, He went with His disciples and a large crowd to a city called Nain. As they approached the city, a large crowd came out towards them carrying a dead man, the only son of his mother, who was also a widow. As these two crowds came together, Jesus told the mother not to weep and then commanded the young man to arise. In the presence of these two large groups, the young man sat up and was returned to his mother. The response of all who saw was to glorify God and say, "A great prophet has risen up among us"; and "God has visited His people."

Nearly everywhere Jesus went performing wonderful works He was praised as a great prophet, but Nain was particularly meaningful. The city of Nain was just 1-2 miles from another town well known in Old Testament history as the city of Shunem, where the Lord through his prophet Elisha had raised a young boy from the dead. The city of Shunem is referenced just a few times as a marker in the Old Testament,[1] but it takes prominence in II Kings 4 because Elisha regularly passed through it and met there a notable woman known to history only as the Shunammite woman.

The Shunammite woman is introduced to us as a "notable" woman.[2] The Hebrew word gives the sense of being greatly distinguished among others. While it seems she had considerable means, servants, and land, the extent of her wealth is not known from this passage. The Scripture's focus is on her deeds. She watched out for the Lord's prophet and provided food for him on his journeys. Proverbs 31 speaks of a virtuous woman in this way: "She extends her hand to the poor, yes, she reaches out her hands to the needy...strength and honor are her clothing; she shall rejoice in time to come. She opens her mouth with wisdom, and on her tongue is the law of kindness."

A virtuous woman is difficult to find. The husband of II Kings 4, however, certainly found her. She was notable for her deeds and is remembered for the way in which she cared for the prophet Elisha. He had been used of God to care for a widow and her sons, and when he went to Shunem a woman and her husband cared for him.

It seems today everyone lives for the notoriety of their own name. How many followers does he have? How many likes did she

---

[1] See Joshua 19:18 and I Samuel 28:4.

[2] The NKJV translates this Hebrew word as "notable," the KJV as "great," and the ESV as "wealthy." The text tends to have its primary focus on a comparison of her actions to those of others rather than on her wealth. This does not preclude her from having been a wealthy woman but she used her means for kindness to others.

receive? The spread of your name means little before God. Notable in God's eyes is the one who loves the Lord his God with all his heart, soul, strength, and mind, and his neighbor as himself. Are you a notable man or woman today because you fear and serve the Lord? Do away with the world's foolishness: There is no greater legacy or service than this: "To do justly, to love mercy, and to walk humbly with your God" (Micah 6:8b).

82

Christian Living 101

Now it happened one day that Elisha went to Shunem, where there was a notable woman, and she persuaded him to eat some food. So it was, as often as he passed by, he would turn in there to eat some food. And she said to her husband, "Look now, I know that this is a holy man of God, who passes by us regularly. Please, let us make a small upper room on the wall; and let us put a bed for him there, and a table and a chair and a lamp stand; so it will be, whenever he comes to us, he can turn in there."

II Kings 4:8-10 NKJV

When I started college, I had to take many '101' classes. They were introductory and foundational courses which my education would be built in the following years. In Principles of Finance (Finance 101), we were taught basics such as Assets - Liabilities = Equity. A class on asset valuation or distressed credit would be of little benefit to a student who didn't know how a balance sheet functioned. It seems to me we see a similar concept in the Christian life.

What profit is there in expounding the deep mysteries of the Scripture on various topics such as assurance of salvation and perseverance of the saints if one does not have the foundations of of the Christian life? What are the foundations of Christian living? What does the Christian life look like?

There are many ways we could answer this question but what better answer than that given to us by the Shunammite woman? She was given over to kindness to the Lord's prophet and full of good works. Kindness! What would you think of someone claiming to be a Christian, expounding on the presence of the Lord in the sacrament of the Lord's Supper, who was rude, mean, self-centered, and given to pride? The confession would not match up with the life. A consultant on asset valuation who didn't understand the balance sheet equation would be considered a fraud. What about a Christian who is not given to kindness?

The Shunammite woman fed Elisha, sheltered him, developed a plan to house him and presented it to her husband. "Let each of you look out not only for his own interests, but also for the interests of others" (Philippians 2:4). As she cared for Elisha's physical nourishment with food she began thinking of ways she could provide even further care to the man of God. She did not consider it a burden but seems to have rejoiced in serving the Lord in this way. She was given over to kindness and is notable for this very reason.

If we say kindness is the foundation of Christian living, would we be slipping into moralism? Is mere kindness the essence of Christianity? What about the Mormons, Roman Catholics, Buddhists, and many other religious practices that espouse kindness? Is that all Christianity is? Is that all the Shunammite woman is an example of, moralism? No, the kindness of the Christian is foundational because of its source.

"And be kind to one another, tender hearted, forgiving one another, even as God in Christ forgave you" (Ephesians 4:32). The kindness that was the foundation of the Shunammite woman's care for Elisha was not mere moralism but was a response to a work done within her. Christian kindness is unlike any other kindness because of the reason for which it is shown. The essence of a Christian is that he has been saved from his sins by Christ his Savior. What greater kindness has been showed than this, that Jesus Christ came and died for wretched sinners such as me? No greater love exists than this, that one would lay down one's life for a friend. And yet Jesus laid down His life while we were still sinning against Him. So the Christian is one who has tasted, seen, experienced, and received this saving kindness of Jesus Christ. In response to such kindness, the Christian is kind to others, tender hearted, forgiving one another.

Because of the kindness of the Lord to the Shunammite woman, she showed kindness to Elisha in a notable way. Because of the kindness of the Lord to the Christian, the Christian must be known for his kindness. If the Christian is not kind to his core, it is not unreasonable to ask if he has received Christ. When someone comes to me asking how to evaluate the credit worthiness of a company, I do not start with discounted cash flow analysis but with the basics of cash, debt, profit, and balance sheets. Before we can go on to the deeper things of the Lord, the foundation must be in place. If one knows not how to be kind, how can one move on to the deeper things of the Lord? Let us learn from the great kindness of this notable woman, "on [whose] tongue is the law of kindness" because she had been forgiven of her sins.

Brothers and sisters, let us "be kind one to another, tender hearted, forgiving one another, even as God in Christ forgave you." This is the foundation of Christian Living.

83

A God Honoring Marriage

Now please, let us make a small upper room on the wall; and let us put a bed for him there, and a table and a chair and a lamp stand; so it will be whenever he comes to us, he can turn in there. And it happened one day that he came there, and he turned in to the upper room and lay down there.

II Kings 4:10-11 NKJV

M any theological matters find their best exposition through parables and historic examples. What is the kingdom of Heaven like? It "is like a merchant seeking beautiful pearls, who, when he found one pearl of great price, went and sold all that he had and bought it" (Matt. 13:45-46). What does it mean to be called to suffer? Christ suffered for us leaving an example ...who, when He was reviled, did not revile in return; when He suffered, He did not threaten, but committed Himself to Him who judges righteously..." (I Peter 2:21-24). How can I know the resurrection on the last day to be true? "But now Christ is risen from the dead, and has become the first fruits of those who have fallen asleep" (I Cor. 15:20).

Few theological topics seem to be more polarizing at present than the topic of men and women, wives and husbands, and their God-ordained roles in this life. In an effort to promote certain terminology that neither the Scripture nor Reformed confessions espouse or ideologies that are in opposition to Scripture, the church has been left unsettled as to the theology of male and female relationships and roles. Many husbands and wives, sessions, and presbyters, have had long discussions on portions of

Scripture unpopular with the world or questionably used in the church.

What does it mean for wives to submit to their own husbands as to the Lord (Eph. 5:22, Col. 3:18, I Peter 3:1-2)? What does it mean for husbands to love their wives as Christ also loved the church (Eph. 5:25) or for husbands to give honor to the wife (I Peter 3:7)? How are we to understand such portions of Scripture in this present evil age? The Lord does not leave us without help, but gives us a living example from a husband and wife whose names we will only know in glory. The wife is of course the Shunammite woman. Her husband is only referred to as "her husband." But together they teach us a great deal about the way God has ordained for husbands and wives in particular to be kind to one another, tender hearted, forgiving one another.

Notice first the reverence, respect, and submissiveness that the Shunammite woman had for her husband. She was a very wise woman, "notable" in the land. "She opens her mouth with wisdom, and on her tongue is the law of kindness" (Prov. 31:26). She saw a way to consider the needs of Elisha and care for them. She made a plan (vs. 10), she gave a godly basis for her request (vs. 9), and she did not demand it of her husband but asked him to do this not for her but with her: "Please, let us make a small upper room on the wall..." (vs. 10). Wives, submit yourselves to your husbands; look to the Shunammite woman.

Next, notice the love, honor, and cherishing of the husband for his wife. He loved her as he loved himself. So great is the honor bestowed by the husband on the wife that we do not read of any debate or argument or concern; "the heart of her husband safely trusts in her... he praises her," for she was a woman who feared the Lord. By the text's next sentence the room has been made (vs. 11). The silence of the Scripture speaks volumes to the relationship and love of husband and wife. The husband, as we will see again in vs.' 22-25, trusted her and honored her wishes, loving her even as himself.

Finally, as the Shunammite woman submitted to and reverence's her husband, and the husband loved and honored the wife, together in this God ordained marriage they honored, glorified, and enjoyed the Lord. One day, the man of God, Elisha, turned in to the upper room and lay down there (vs. 11).

Here is the very picture of a God glorifying marriage that was used for the advancement and benefit of the kingdom of God. In serving the Lord and living together according to the Word of God, this husband and wife glorified God and were profitable servants in His kingdom. We can waste our hours and days in contention as husbands and wives or we can submit ourselves to the Word of God and the service of Christ as He has called us to do. Perhaps the lack of the latter practice has created the problems we now face as a church. If we live before the Lord in our marriages as the Shunammite woman and her husband, perhaps these theological issues will once again be clear and matters of peace in Christ's kingdom.

84

Godliness With Contentment

Then he said to Gehazi his servant, "Call this Shunammite woman.'"When he called her, she stood before him. And he said to him, "Say now to her, Look, you have been concerned for us with all this care. What can I do for you? Do you want me to speak on your behalf to the king or to the commander of the army?'" She answered, "I dwell among my own people."

II Kings 4:12-13 NKJV

What would you do if someone close to the President of the United States came to you and asked if there was anything you would like to request of or say to the President? If you are at all like me, perhaps you could think of 5-10 things in a matter of seconds. The opportunity to have the ear of someone in power is rare for the majority of people and it would be very desirable to take full advantage of if.

The Shunammite woman had shown kindness to Elisha and his servant Gehazi. Elisha, desiring to honor the Lord and repay the kindness in some way, called the Shunammite woman to him and asked, "What can I do for you?"

Elisha had stood before great kings and generals. He had their ear. He could make a request before the king on behalf of this woman from Shunem and have reasonable expectation the thing would be done. Surely there was something the Shunammite woman would desire for Elisha to say to or request of the king or general.

After several verses exemplifying the virtues of this godly woman, yet another virtue is demonstrated in her interaction with Elisha. She was a woman of great humility and contentment. In her opportunity to have sway over the leaders of Israel, her response was simply, "I dwell among my own people." Matthew Henry expounds on her statement in this way, "It is a happiness to dwell among our own people, that love and respect us, and to whom we are in a capacity of doing good; and a greater happiness to be content to do so, to be easy, and to know when we are well off. Why should those that live comfortably among their own people covet to live delicately in kings' palaces?"

Some years later the Shunammite woman would have need of the king's lawful assistance and would turn to him for help (II Kings 8:1-6). But in the special favor Elisha was offering she was content in serving the Lord where He had put her.

"Godliness with contentment is great gain" (I Tim. 6:6). The Shunammite woman had gained contentment. In the courts of men, there was nothing for which the Shunammite woman had need, for the Lord had satisfied her soul with the great treasure of contentment.

The Lord has given us that which we need most by giving us the Messiah who is Christ the Lord. In contrast to the Lord Jesus Christ, all else is but rubbish. Eternal life and salvation is found in Christ alone; all else is quickly perishing. With this truth set before us, may we run the Christian race with contentment in all situations. Whether the Lord see fits to give us much or little, a life of public influence or a life of quietness, may we bless the name of the Lord and offer our thanks to Him.

85

The Lord Gives

So he said, 'What then is to be done for her?" And Gehazi
answered, "Actually, she has no son, and her husband is old." So he
said, "Call her" When he had called her, she stood in the doorway.
Then he said, "About this time next year you shall embrace a son."
And she said, "No my lord. Man of God, do not lie to your
maidservant!'" But the woman conceived, and bore a son when
the appointed time had come, of which Elisha had told her.

II Kings 4:14-17 NKJV

In I Kings 3 the Lord appeared to Solomon and asked him, "What shall I give you?" Solomon asked for wisdom, "an understanding heart to judge Your people..." Because Solomon asked for that which was good instead of asking for things of the world, such as riches and honor, the Lord promised to give Solomon wisdom, riches, and honor. Solomon became one of the wisest of all men and abundant in riches and honor, so that royalty came from far away to hear the wisdom of Solomon and admire the beauty of his kingdom.

The Shunammite woman did not ask anything from the courts of this world, for there was nothing that she needed from them. Thanks to the providence of God in the perception of Gehazi, Elisha went to the courts of heaven for the Shunammite woman when he heard she had no son. So Elisha called her and gave her a promise from the Lord: She would have a son in about a year.

This reminds us of Sarah who was promised a son in her old age and Hannah who was barren and prayed for a child from the Lord.

So this woman had an old husband[1] and seemed unlikely to conceive, and yet the Lord was going to give her a son.

The response of the woman shows her knowledge of both Elisha and of her current situation. She responded with respect and recognition of Elisha's office but also with disbelief: "No, my lord. Man of God, do not lie to your maidservant!" The thing was too good to be true, was she being mocked? He who had caused other women's barren womb's to bear in the past was certainly able to give her a son whose husband was old. And so the Lord did as He promised and at the appointed time the Lord gave the woman a son.

"Every good gift and every perfect gift is from above, and comes down from the Father of lights, with whom there is no variation or shadow of turning" (James 1:17). As you look around at your home, your vehicles, your clothing, your worldly possessions, your children, parents, and siblings, do you consider where those gifts come from? The Lord is the giver of them all. Perhaps we see this most evidently in the gift of children. The Lord is the giver of life and the fruit of the womb is His reward. Let us give thanks today for the many good gifts the Lord has given to us.

---

[1] The text does not tell us that the Shunammite woman was old but only that her husband was old. While it is possible she was also old the focus of the text is on the age of the husband rather than that of the wife. In either event, there were natural prohibitions from another child for this family.

86

The Lord Takes Away

And the child grew. Now it happened one day that he went out to his father, to the reapers. And he said to his father, 'My head, my head!' So he said to a servant, 'Carry him to his mother.' When he had taken him and brought him to his mother, he sat on her knees till noon, and then died.

II Kings 4:18-20 NKJV

There is an interesting phrase between the parentheses of answer 66 of the Westminster Shorter Catechism: "The reason annexed to the fifth commandment is, a promise of long life and prosperity **(as far as it shall serve for God's glory and their own good)** to all such as keep this commandment." (Bold added for emphasis)

The fifth commandment is referred to in Ephesians 5:2 as the "first commandment with promise." The general promise is a long life on Earth. But God, who is rich in mercy, abundant in grace, and full of truth, may design a child's life to be cut short on earth for His own glory and our good.[1] What if God, desiring to bring a child to Himself early, direct his parents, siblings, and friends all the more to trust in the Lord; and increase the faith and witness of His church, takes someone we love dearly and brings him from this life to glory sooner than we would expect?

---

[1] Consider the Israelite children in Egypt (Exodus 1:15-22), David's son (II Samuel 12:15-23), the widow of Zarephath's son , the infant sons of Bethlehem in the days of Herod (Matt. 2:16-18), Jairus's daughter (Mark 5:38); and the widow of Nain's son (Luke 7:11-17).

This is precisely what happened to the Shunammite. She had been given a son by the special gift of the Lord. After that great blessing, a day came when those fateful words were heard by the father from the mouth of his son, "My head, my head!"

The boy was still alive when he was brought home to his mother where she comforted him, cared for him, held him on her knees until noon, and then watched helplessly as he died in her arms. The gift of the Lord, taken away without warning, with nothing his parents could do to prevent it. What terrible anguish it is for the family who loses a child. There are rarely answers to the questions we direct to the Lord and to ourselves: Why? How? For what purpose?

When Job heard of the loss of his ten children at one time, he fell down to the ground and worshipped, making this confession: "Naked I came from my mother's womb, and naked shall I return there. The Lord gave, and the Lord has taken away..."

The Shunammite's son was not taken away by an enemy. The Shunammite's son was taken away by the same one who gave her her son. The Lord gave him to her, and the Lord took him away.

Sometimes it does not serve for God's glory to grant long life to us or someone dear to us. Yet we have this truth we must hold dear: "Not one [sparrow] falls to the ground apart from your Father's will. But the very hairs of your head are all numbered. Do not fear therefore; you are of more value than many sparrows" (Matthew 10:29-30). The Lord takes us away. The Lord is sovereign over our life, and may we also trust Him who is sovereign over the day of our death.

87

Blessed Be the Name of the Lord!

And she went up and laid him on the bed of the man of God, shut the door upon him, and went out. Then she called to her husband, and said, "Please send me one of the young men and one of the donkeys, that I may run to the man of God and come back." So he said, "Why are you going to him today? It is neither the new moon nor the Sabbath." And she said, "It is Well."

II Kings 4:21-23 NKJV

Where may we run to in the day of adversity? Should we run to the hills to hide? Should we run to the leaders of the world for protection? Should we run to our financial assets to acquire safety? Should we run to false gods and idols to answer the desires of our hearts?

The Shunammite woman had just lost her young and only son. He died in her arms. She gently laid him down in Elisha's room and then turned her attention to one thing, to the Lord and His prophet Elisha. She intended to go quickly to the man of God; she would not stop to mourn but would run to him.

She asked her husband to lend her one of the family's employees and donkeys that she might make the greatest speed possible to reach Elisha, the man of God. Her husband, thinking she intended to offer a sacrifice and worship God at this time, asked her why she must go seeing as it was not the day of worship (the Sabbath), nor was it a separate special day of worship (the new moon). Both the husband and the wife had their hearts at this grievous time on the blessing and worship of the Lord.

As Job spoke those memorable words that we visited in the last devotional, he did not end with "The Lord gave, and the Lord has taken away..." but he continued, "Blessed be the name of the Lord."

I have had occasion to observe several unbelievers respond to tragedy and unexpected death. The responses vary but often include loud cursing, anger, and rage. Others respond almost completely opposite with no words at all... and no hope. It is a terrible thing to face loss without the Lord because it is a reminder of the spiritual state apart from the Lord.

Though Christians grieve, mourn, and lament deeply the losses they experience in this life, it is not a grieving without hope. For though great loss transpires and suffering occurs, and they will for the Christian, yet the Lord our God cannot be taken from us. So we grieve as those with hope in the Lord and bless the name of the Lord.

At the hour of great need, the Shunammite woman went to the place of help, she would go to the prophet of the Lord who would reveal to her the very word of the Lord. Where do you go in your days of adversity and need? "My help comes from the LORD, who made heaven and earth" (Psalm 121:2).

88

"It Is Well"

So he said, "Why are you going to him today? It is neither the new moon nor the Sabbath." And she said, "It is well."

II Kings 4:23 NKJV

Horatio Spafford was a successful businessman from Chicago. He and his wife Anna had five children, a son and four daughters. Their only son died of pneumonia at a young age. Later they lost their business to the Chicago fire. In 1873, Anna and the four daughters were on an ocean liner heading towards Europe while Horatio stayed behind a few days to finish some business. The ladies' ship collided with another vessel and in 12 minutes the ship had sunk taking 226 passengers, including all four Spafford daughters, down with it. Anna was found holding on to a piece of wreckage and eventually made it to Wales where she sent the following message to her husband, "Saved alone, what shall I do?"

Mr. Spafford immediately left to join his grieving wife in Wales and while on the voyage he penned the words to the hymn known today, "It Is Well With My Soul." The Spaffords' would go on to have three more children, one of whom would also die of pneumonia.

When the Shunammite woman was preparing to go to Elisha her husband asked her about the timing. Although he was concerned for her in the loss of their child and the timing of the actions she was taking, she responded with only these three words which we know so well from Mr. Spafford's hymn, "It is well."

How is it that after losing her only son perhaps just minutes before, she could tell her husband, "It is well"? Commentators have given different opinions, some suggesting she was brushing off her husband's question, even suggesting the words meant "never mind" instead of "it is well". Others have suggested she was too overcome to say anything else but this contradicts the previous verse when she was able to prepare for a trip to Elisha.

We have in the Shunammite woman a great example of faith in the Lord her God so was she just brushing off her husband or was she communicating something else?

First, the Hebrew word translated "it is well" in the NKJV is the well known Hebrew word, Shalom. It means more than just peace, but also contentment and safety, and it suggests to others that they should be satisfied regarding the speaker's welfare. The Shunammite woman was at peace, it was well with her for one reason, the Lord God Almighty was with her! Nothing could destroy her so long as the Lord was with her and He was.

Second, it was well with the Shunammite woman because her son was with the Lord! Can there be greater loss than the loss of one's child? It is hard to imagine any. But can there be greater peace than knowing one's child is safe in the arms of the Lord of Lords and King of Kings? It was well with the Shunammite woman because her son was well with the Lord.

Third, it was well with the Shunammite because she hoped in God as the Resurrection and the Life. Throughout the Old Testament we see a perfect assurance of Christians in the ability of God to raise the dead in their day and the assurance of the resurrection at the last day.[1]

For these reasons, when Gehazi came to the Shunammite woman in verse 26 asking "Is it well with you? Is it well with your husband? Is it well with the child?... she answered, "It is well."

Mrs. Spafford said after the death of her daughters, "God gave me four daughters. Now they have been taken from me. Someday I will understand why." That perfect assurance in the Lord made it well with her soul and the soul of her husband. It was well with the Shunammite, for the Lord was her, her son was with the Lord, and the Lord has the power to raise the dead. Jesus said in John 11, "I am the resurrection and the life. He who believes in Me, though he may die, he shall live. And whoever lives and believes in Me shall never die. Do you believe this?" Is it well with your soul today?[2]

---

[1] Abraham concluded that God was able to raise Isaac up, even from the dead (Hebrews 11:19). David prophesied that "God will redeem my soul from the power of the grave, for He shall receive me" (Psalm 49:15). See also Psalm 71:20. Several prophets prophesied to this truth, though the clearest examples came after the Shunammite woman's life (Daniel 12:2; Isaiah 26:19, Ezekiel 37).

[2] The background details of the Spafford story were taken from memory and from *The St. Augustine Record* (staugustine.com), "Story behind the song: It is well with my soul." Published October 16, 2014 by Ph.D.

When peace like a river attendeth my way
When sorrows like sea billows roll
Whatever my lot thou hast taught me to say
It is well, It is well with my soul

Though Satan should buffet, though trials should come
Let this blest assurance control
That Christ has regarded my helpless estate
And has shed His own blood for my soul

My sin, O the bliss, of this glorious thought
My sin, not in part, but the whole
Is nailed to the cross and I bear it no more
Praise the Lord, Praise the Lord, O my soul

O Lord haste the day when the faith shall be sight
The clouds be rolled back as a scroll
The trump shall resound and the Lord shall descend
Even so, it is well, with my soul.

~Horatio Spafford

89

Relentless Determination

Then she saddled a donkey, and said to her servant, "Drive, and go forward; do not slacken the pace unless I tell you. And so she departed, and went to the man of God at Mt. Carmel. So it was, when the man of God saw her afar off, that he said to his servant Gehazi, "Look, the Shunammite woman! Please run now to meet her, and say to her, "Is it well with you? Is it well with your husband? Is it well with the child?" And she answered, "It is well."

II Kings 4:24 - 26 NKJV

How earnestly do you pursue the knowledge of the Lord, the power of His resurrection, the fellowship of His sufferings, the conformation to His death, so that by any means possible you might attain to the resurrection from the dead? When Paul uses these words in Philippians 3:10-11 he prefaces them by saying he counts "all things as loss for the excellence of the knowledge of Christ Jesus my Lord." Paul expands this by saying he counts all things as rubbish (literally, dung) that he might gain Christ and be found in Him. Forgetting what lies behind and reaching for the things ahead, "I press toward the goal for the prize of the upward call of God in Christ Jesus."

The Shunammite's determination to see the will of the Lord through Elisha was relentless. Nothing would get in her way. She would not let the roughness of the road, the pain to her body, nor the weariness of the journey stop her until she was with the man of God at Mount Carmel. Have we ever seen faith like this?

The haste of the Shunammite's journey was noticeable from a great distance. Certainly the dust and perhaps the noise of the carriage at great speed also alerted Elisha to her approach, and he recognized the Shunammite woman. Her relentless determination uphill towards the summit of a mountain no less caught the attention of the prophet of God who would see to her well-being. Elisha sent Gehazi to inquire of her as we considered last time, and the Shunammite confirmed it was well before coming to Elisha himself.

The Shunammite woman would not rest until she had seen Elisha. Her godly mission would not be hindered by physical pain or natural barrier. By any means possible, with all her strength, she would come before the prophet of the Lord at Mt. Carmel, the mountain of the Lord's great power.

Do you and I have such determination to come before the Lord? Do we run the Christian race like this Shunammite did, not looking back to the ease of the world, not looking aside for relief from the present distress, but looking ahead to that One from whom our help comes, to the Lord God Almighty? Christ has gained Heaven for us but we are not yet in heaven. We are not yet perfected, Paul says, because we are not yet in glory. So press on that you may lay hold of that eternal life that is yours only because Christ Jesus has made you His own. Run the Christian race. Pursue the prize of the upward call of Christ. Remember the relentless pursuit of the Shunammite woman and pursue the Lord and the power of His resurrection after her example and that of Paul.

Run that you may win Christ!

90

Humility in the Hour of Need

Now when she came to the man of God at the hill, she caught him by the feet, but Gehazi came near to push her away. But the man of God said, "Let her alone; for her soul is in deep distress, and the LORD has hidden it from me, and has not told me."

II Kings 4:27 NKJV

Imagine if someone came to you, fell down with their head bowed, and took hold of your feet. This is one of the greatest postures of humility or reverence that can be shown to someone. This was a constant occurrence in Jesus's life as people came to Him for help, healing, and forgiveness. The Greek woman, a Syrophoenician by birth, whose daughter had a demon came and fell at Jesus feet.[1] Jairus came to Jesus when his daughter had died and fell at His feet.[2] When the one leper in ten, a Samaritan, returned to thank Jesus he fell down on his face at His feet to worship Him.[3] In the Old Testament, when Abigail came to make peace with David for the offenses of Nabal her husband she came to David and fell at his feet in respect.[4]

The Shunammite woman made it to the top of Mount Carmel where she approached Elisha, the man of God. Immediately she caught him by the feet. This was not a sign of the Shunammite worshipping Elisha, but of reverence and also of great need. Holding his feet meant she would not let him go until he had

---

[1] Mark 7:25-26.

[2] Luke 8:41.

[3] Luke 17:16.

[4] I Samuel 25:23-24.

heard and addressed her need. She who had lost her only son went to the man of God for help in her hour of need and went to him with great humility.

Clearly this type of humility was not common for Elisha or Gehazi to see and Gehazi came to push her away. The idea was, 'Who does this woman think she is coming and hindering Elisha's steps by clinging to his feet?' Many will come telling us not to cling to the feet of Christ for salvation. They will want us to look anywhere else but to God who alone can do all things. They will tell us to go back the way we came for the Savior does not want to hear us. But the Shunammite woman held onto the feet of Elisha and would not let him go. In her hour of need, she humbled herself and went to her Lord through His prophet, who is referred to in this section as "the man of God" to make this connection to the Lord very clear in our minds.

The truth of the matter is that our hour of need is every hour. The Lord gives us our breath and if He were to remove His hand from us for just a minute we would be no more. Are you clinging to the feet of Christ? Do you hold fast to His Word of everlasting life with unyielding determination? The Shunammite woman clung to Elisha's feet. She held fast and would not let go until her need was addressed, however that would happen.

Friends, lay hold on Christ Jesus and His word and do not let Him go. He is freely offered to you in His Word. He has all power to save you. The world will seek to pull you away with every distraction and sin imaginable, do not let go! Come before Him in prayer and with humility. Fall down at His feet, for the one who comes to Him, He will by no means cast out.[5]

---

[5] John 6:37.

91

A Man of God... but Not God

Now when she came to the man of God at the hill, she caught him by the feet, but Gehazi came near to push her away. But the man of God said, "Let her alone; for her soul is in deep distress, and the LORD has hidden it from me, and has not told me."

II Kings 4:27 NKJV

One of the many great deceits that has been propagated in the Roman Catholic Church is the idea that Mary and the Roman Catholic saints are all-knowing (omniscient) or at least all-hearing. This is linked with another great deceit that calls Roman Catholics to pray to Mary and other dead saints for help and mercy in direct contradiction with the Word of God, which teaches us to pray to God only. There is none who knows all things but God only who alone has infinite knowledge. All other knowledge is finite. Consider even the great prophet Elisha, the man of God. The Lord had told and revealed much to him, but the reason for the relentless driving of the Shunammite woman from Shunem all the way up Mount Carmel to the feet of Elisha had been hidden from him. The Lord had not told Elisha the matter that was now before him; He had not told him that the Shunammite's son had died. Elisha was a man of God, but Elisha was not God.

As we have seen in the past, so we will see in the future, that the prophets of the Lord, while great in wisdom and power from on high, were still limited in their ability and understanding and relied on the Lord to provide all of their wisdom and strength. On the very mountain where Elisha, Gehazi, and the Shunammite woman now stood, Elijah had prayed and God sent the fire down from Heaven.

What a contrast we see between Elisha and the greatest prophet, Jesus Christ. Elisha did not know all things. Jesus knew all things and was able to do all things of His own power. When the Pharisees grumbled in the back of the room in Mark 2 at Jesus telling the man with the palsy that his sins were forgiven, Jesus who knows all things perceived the reasoning of the Pharisees and spoke to them, chastising them for their unbelieving thoughts. He knew what was in the heart of men to tempt Him. He saw Nathaniel under the fig tree, long before Nathaniel stood before His presence (John 1:43-47). How was Jesus the prophet of God able to know all these things and Elisha not able? Elisha was a man of God but Jesus is the God-Man!

Why would anyone consider praying to someone dead? Why would anyone consider praying to someone who does not know all things? All who pray to dead saints pray to those who cannot hear them, let alone answer them. But you who believe in Jesus Christ alone for salvation have not come to such a miserable state. You have not come to Mount Sinai or Mount Carmel or any other mountain that may be touched. You have not come to a mere human prophet who knows not all things and will one day die as did Elisha. But you have come to Mount Zion, and to the city of the living God, the heavenly Jerusalem, to Jesus the mediator. Scripture does not call Jesus "a" mediator as if He were one of many, but the article "the" denotes "only." "For there is one God and one Mediator between God and men, the Man Christ Jesus, who gave Himself a ransom for all..." (I Tim 2:5-6).

In the Old Testament, it was proper for people to go to the men of God for help from God. But in the New Testament, we have been given an even better testimony and access to God. We need not go through mere men but we have access directly to the God-Man Jesus Christ. Go to Him for help, He knows all things and can do all things, and none who ask will He turn away.

92

Godly Grief

So she said, "Did I ask a son of my lord? Did I not say, "Do not deceive me?"

II Kings 4:28 NKJV

For many years Job enjoyed prosperity, peace, and joy on a level few in history have experienced. He was not prideful about his 10 children, 7,000 sheep, 3,000 camels, 500 yoke of oxen, and 500 donkeys, but would go often to worship and sacrifice before the Lord who had shown such great kindness to him. What are we to make of the removal of these blessings by the Lord for a time? Job fell down in dust and ashes and worshipped the Lord. The Shunammite rushed to the mountain of God and His prophet to discern the reason for the Lord's providence in her life.

When she was finally able to speak she poured out her heart before Elisha and the Lord: "Did I ask for a son of my Lord?" Remember that in her humility, the Shunammite asked for nothing from Elisha in return for the kindness that she had shown to him. So Elisha told her she would be blessed with a son (vs. 16) who was a great gift and mercy from God but now was dead. 'I did not ask for this mercy but you gave it and now have taken it away. Why?'

She then reminded Elisha that she had not wanted to be deceived with the news of a coming child. It was too good to be true to have a son at this time in life and She did not want to be crushed if it turned out to be a false hope. And it all came to pass as Elisha had prophesied. She had a son. But now the child was dead. The mercy of the Lord seemed to have been removed. In her grief she turned to Elisha and said in essence, "Isn't this the one thing I asked you not to do... do not deceive me?" Do not cause my joy to be turned into sorrow like it has now. Did you bring my son to me only to give me more sorrow in his death than the joy I had in his life?"

These thoughts are not unknown to those who read this and have experienced losses of their own. Echos of Psalm 77 come to mind when the psalmist asks of God, "Has His mercy ceased forever? Has His promise failed forevermore? Has God forgotten to be gracious? Has He in anger shut up His tender mercies?" How could God give such mercy, such a gift and then take it away?

Matthew Henry says this, "The loss of mercy should not make us undervalue the gift of it... The providence of God may disappoint us, we may be sure the promise of God never did, nor ever will, deceive us..." What are we then to make of the loss of God's gift?

As we experience griefs and sorrows of life, let us do so while remembering the years of the right hand of the Most High. Remember the works of the Lord. Remember His wonders of old. Meditate on all His deeds. Talk about all of His works. He who gives such wonderful gifts will not destroy us by taking them away but will bring glory to His name. Life is a gift from God which He may take away, but He has given us His Word that we might know something of Him. He has comforted the grieving. He has raised the dead. He has forgiven sinners. And He will surely do it again. As we grieve, may the Lord enable us to grieve with hope in the Lord who has been faithful from the beginning and will in no way cease to be faithful in the present trial.

93

Relics of Little Value

"Then he said to Gehazi, "Get yourself ready, and take my staff in your hand, and be on your way. If you meet anyone, do not greet him; and if anyone greets you, do not answer him; but lay my staff on the face of the child." And the mother of the child said, "As the LORD lives, and as your soul lives, I will not leave you." So he arose and followed her. Now Gehazi went on ahead of them, and laid the staff on the face of the child; but there was neither voice nor hearing. Therefore he went back to meet him, and told him, saying, "The child was not awakened.""

II Kings 4:29-31 NKJV

In 2019, a procession went down the streets of NYC, led by Cardinal Timothy Dolan of the Roman Catholic Church with the focus on a box that contained the "incorrupt" (undecomposed) heart of a French saint who had died more than 150 years earlier. It traveled through NYC so that it could be venerated by faithful Roman Catholics on its way to St. Patrick's Cathedral. The Black Nazarene is a life-sized crucifix that is the most famous relic of the Philippines. Most Roman Catholics in the Philippines believe that just by touching it one can be healed of diseases. An elaborate scheme has been established by Rome over the centuries to grant power, status, and indulgences in and through relics. Rome has even ordained official "Curators of the Relics" authorized to designate such items as relics for veneration. The highest prized relics are body parts of dead saints, with heads, hearts, brains, fingers, and ears taking high places in the lives of relic venerators. To give the practice the semblance of true Christianity, papists are told the relics have no power other than to bring people closer to God through their veneration.

The problems with this practice and the theology behind it are manifold and far outside the scope of a devotional. Suffice it to say throughout Scripture the Lord forbids His people from worshipping or approaching Him in or through images or any way not appointed in His Word so that to venerate an image is to rob God of the glory due to Him alone. The Pope and his priests, highly decorated in all manner of gold and ostentatious displays of papal wealth, have ordained and established the veneration and power of relics in opposition to God's Word and sadly the followers of these men have followed suit (Acts 17:22-33).

What then of Elisha's staff?

Elisha gave his staff to Gehazi to lay on the dead son of the Shunammite woman. This staff was no replication but the real thing. It didn't pass thousands of years through mysterious circumstances to leave Gehazi with a mere splinter of wood claimed by some wise merchant of Jericho to be the staff of a famous prophet; it was the very staff of Elisha himself. Surely if there were ever a relic that had power it would be the staff of Elisha. But with the staff laid upon him the child was did not awaken (vs. 31).

In an unusual comment for Matthew Henry he says of verse 29, "I know not what to make of this…" Why did Elisha send Gehazi with his staff? Was Elisha not remembering to seek the wisdom of the Lord? Was Elisha trusting in his own power instead of the Lord's? Was Elisha doubting the reality of death in the Shunammite woman's son? Scripture does not give us the answer to the question, "Why?" But it does reveal this: There is no power in created man or objects to raise the dead but in God alone.

Put no confidence in princes, prophets, wood, stone, undecomposed hearts, decomposed hearts, fingers, brains, splinters, crying statues, paintings, beads, necklaces, or anything else that may be offered, sold, or suggested to you - put your trust in the Lord!

Elisha's staff did nothing for the woman or her son. Dear friend, if you are in the church of Rome or of Eastern, Greek, Russian, or any other "Orthodoxy" with a country's name in front of it, may the Word of God enlight your mind and heart today with a truth that will never grow dim. All the hopes of the world are idols and foolishness but he who hopes in the Lord will never be ashamed.

If you are going through great trials today - fears, grief, uncertainty, illness, pain, whatever the case may be - and your hope is in the Lord, do not take your eyes off of Him! He will be your guide and Lord from this time forth and forevermore. One day, the faith you placed solely in Jesus Christ will be vindicated in the eyes of all the world, for the Lord Jesus Christ shall descend with a shout, with the voice of the archangel, with the trumpet of the Lord, and all flesh shall see Him together when those who put their trust in the Lord are separated from those who put their trust in foolish objects, even if they are holding a splinter from the very cross itself. "Happy is he who has the God of Jacob for his help, whose hope is in the LORD his God" (Psalm 146:5).

94

Her Abiding Faith

And the mother of the child said, "As the LORD lives, and as your soul lives, I will not leave you." So he arose and followed her.

II Kings 4:30 NKJV

When Jesus heard the words and expression of faith from the centurion whose servant was sick, Matthew tells us Jesus "marveled and said to those who followed, 'Assuredly, I say to you, I have not found such great faith, not even in Israel'" (8:10). Who had such faith in Israel in Elisha's day?

After Elisha sent Gehazi to lay his staff on the dead boy, the Shunammite woman did not return to her husband and home. She stayed with Elisha and said, "As the LORD lives, and as your soul lives, I will not leave you." We have come across these words previously in our studies in II Kings. They were the very words used by Elisha before Elijah was taken up into Heaven. We might not marvel at Elisha the prophet speaking them to another prophet who soon would be taken up into glory, but what of a Shunammite woman whose son just died? What faith was there in Israel in Elisha's day like the faith of the Shunammite woman? Hers was an abiding faith.

The word abiding has to do with enduring or remaining. He who endures in the faith until the end will be saved. So the writer of Hebrews gives us God's word saying, "Let us run with endurance the race that is set before us, looking unto Jesus, the author and finisher of our faith, who for the joy that was set before Him endured the cross, despising the shame, and has sat down at the right hand of the throne of God" (Heb. 12:1-3).

Did the Shunammite woman know the words of Elisha on the day Elijah ascended into Heaven? I do not know. But this we can see: Her eyes were fixed on one hope, her Savior, the Messiah, Jehovah God, who would help her. He had begun the faith within her by His free gift and He would surely perfect and finish that faith until the day she saw Him in glory. She could not leave the one with whom the Lord dwelt in a special manner, His prophet, but as long as the Lord lived and as long as Elisha lived, she would be with him until the matter was resolved. What faith in God displayed in this woman and what a response to her faith by Elisha: "So he arose and followed her."

This is a moving portion of Scripture. Elisha would not leave Elijah until the matter was resolved. Now the Shunammite will not leave Elisha until the matter with her son is resolved. Would the Lord raise him now or in the future? Elisha saw this faith and went with her.[1]

How is your faith enduring today? The unrelenting things we see around us are attacks on our faith. Is your faith holding strong? One way to gauge its strength is by examining the foundation. If your foundation is on worldly things, yourself, your strength, your wealth, or your health (perhaps this one is quickly going away?), your faith will not endure because your foundation will not endure. It is like a man who builds his house on the sand. The wind and rain comes and the house falls with a great crash. Conversely, if your faith is in the Lord Jesus Christ by whom you have received and on whom alone you rest for salvation, your faith may be strengthened by attendance to the Word, the

---

[1]Elisha's following gives assent to the idea that Elisha knew Gehazi and the staff would do nothing for the dead boy. It seems the Lord through the prophet may have been testing the faith of the Shunammite woman to see if she would continue in her unrelenting hope in the Lord... and she did.

sacraments, and prayer, and your faith may endure as you keep your eyes on Christ. It is like a man who built his house on the rock. The wind came, the rain fell, and the house stood firm because its foundation was solid rock. Christian, your rock is Christ!

95

Zarephath and Shunem vs. Nain

When Elisha came into the house there was the child, lying dead on his bed. He went in therefore, shut the door behind the two of them, and prayed to the LORD. And he went up and lay on the child, and put his mouth on his mouth, his eyes on his eyes, and his hands on his hands; and he stretched himself out on the child, and the flesh of the child became warm. He returned and walked back and forth in the house and again went up and stretched himself out on him; then the child sneezed seven times, and the child opened his eyes. And he called Gehazi and said, "Call this Shunammite woman." So he called her. And when she came in to him, he said, "Pick up your son."

II Kings 4:32-36 NKJV

Hardly a living person would disagree with the statement "Jesus was a great man!" Many would, however, disagree with the statement "Jesus is the God Man." When the Jehovah's Witnesses or Mormons knock on your door they typically promote Jesus verbally and through their own literature and want their audience to think of their practice as "Christian." But as you talk with them about their Jesus, it takes little time to recognize that the Jesus they promote is simply an idol and not the Jesus of Scripture who lives and reigns even now and will soon come from Heaven to judge the living and the dead. The Jesus they promote and the Jesus many admire today was a mere man like you and I and the great prophets of old.[1]

---

[1]We have seen in previous devotionals that many in Jesus's day thought that Jesus was a great man, but a mere man. "Some say John the Baptist, some Elijah, and others Jeremiah or one of the prophets" (Matthew 16:14).

What is the difference between the Jesus of the Bible and you, me, and the prophets of old? Is there a difference? The histories of the widow of Zarephath and the Shunammite woman are very beneficial for teaching us about the person and work of Jesus Christ. These woman were friends of two of the greatest of the Old Testament prophets, Elijah and Elisha. They both witnessed their sons die. Both saw their sons raised from the dead. Let us consider briefly the means the Lord used to demonstrate His power over life and death in these two women's sons.

"So [Elijah] took him out of her arms and carried him to the upper room where he was staying, and laid him on his own bed. Then he cried out to the LORD and said... 'O Lord my God, I pray, let this child's soul come back to him.' Then the Lord heard the voice of Elijah; and the soul of the child came back to him..." (I Kings 17:19-22).

"When Elisha came into the house, there was the child, lying dead on his bed. He went in therefore, shut the door behind the two of them, and prayed to the LORD...then the child opened his eyes..." (II Kings 4:32-36).

In the hour of need both Elijah and Elisha went to the Lord in prayer. They did not have any power in themselves to raise the children from the dead. In both instances, the Lord heard and answered their prayers and raised the children.

Didn't Jesus also raise the dead? What is the difference then? Let us consider again the widow of Nain (Luke 7:11-17). The two crowds of people, mourners and disciples, met outside the gate of Nain. Jesus had compassion on the widow: "Then He came and touched the open coffin, and those who carried him stood still. And He said, Young man, I say to you, arise! So he who was dead sat up and began to speak" (Luke 7:14-15).

Like the great prophets of old, Jesus ministered to a woman who lost her only son. That is where the similarity ends. In contrast to the prophets of old, Jesus did not pray to ask God to raise the dead. Jesus spoke to the young man and told him, in His own name, to "arise!" Jesus had and has power in, of, and through Himself to command the dead to rise and they obey Him. Jesus has authority and power that no prophet ever had. Who can command life to return to a child but the one who gave the life and took it away? The Lord God is the giver of life. The Lord God takes away life. The Lord God will raise all lives at the last day. No one has power to speak to a dead man and raise him from the dead but God only.

Has anyone ever told you something like this: "Jesus never said He was God?" Such a fallacy can simply be refuted with these words: "The whole of Scripture is testifying to this truth: Jesus was and Jesus is the LORD God." Bring them to Zarephath. Bring them to Shunem. Then bring them to Nain. He who made all things, breaths the breath of life into man, and raises the dead to life, He alone is God and worthy of all adoration, belief, and worship. His name is Jesus and He came to save His people from their sins.

96

The Child Opened His Eyes

When Elisha came into the house there was the child, lying dead on his bed. He went in therefore, shut the door behind the two of them, and prayed to the LORD. And he went up and lay on the child, and put his mouth on his mouth, his eyes on his eyes, and his hands on his hands; and he stretched himself out on the child, and the flesh of the child became warm. He returned and walked back and forth in the house and again went up and stretched himself out on him; then the child sneezed seven times, and the child opened his eyes. And he called Gehazi and said, "Call this Shunammite woman." So he called her. And when she came in to him, he said, "Pick up your son."

II Kings 4:33-36 NKJV

I remember hearing story a while ago about a minister who taught many interns during his years of ministry. On the intern's first day the minister did not bring him into his study or share with him the secrets of godly preaching but instead gave him a toilet brush, brought him to the restrooms and told him to get to work cleaning them. A servant of God cannot be profitable if he is unwilling to roll up his sleeves and serve God's people and Christ's church according to their needs but only according to his desires.

The Shunammite woman would not leave Elisha so Elisha willingly went with her from Mt. Carmel to her house in Shunem where he saw her son, dead and lying on his bed. This journey was not too lowly a task for him but was according to the work God had called him to as a servant. Upon his arrival in Shunem, Elisha immediately shut the door so that he was alone with the boy and prayed to the Lord. Elisha was not making a show of his prayers but needed to be alone with the boy and the Lord so that his mind might be focused. It is wise for all of us when we pray to go alone to our rooms to make our prayers before the Lord.

The Lord did not immediately act and Elisha, under the inspiration of the Lord, lay on top of the child, whose flesh became warm. When Elisha did this a second time the child sneezed seven times and opened his eyes. The effectual fervent prayer of a righteous man again availed much, and the child who was dead was raised by the Lord from the dead.

The Scripture rightly teaches us not to pray for the dead or to the dead. But we are to go to the Lord in prayer and ask Him to raise the dead. When we pray the second petition, "Thy kingdom come," part of that petition is to ask God to hasten the kingdom of glory. That means simply to ask God to come quickly and raise the dead to everlasting glory with Him forever. As we remain constant in prayer to the Lord asking Him to return and raise the dead, one day at last we shall see Him do just that even as He raised the boy in Shunem.

Elisha's instruction to the Shunammite woman can seem somewhat subtle, "Pick up your son," but he is saying something more profound: Come see what the Lord has done for you and your son! Come behold the wondrous works of the Lord your God who caused the eyes of the boy that once were shut in death to be opened again in life. Prayer may seem boring, few will see it, if done in private nobody will commend you for it, but as Elisha privately prayed to the Lord, a dead child was given his life again. Serve the Lord with gladness, gladly go wherever the Lord calls you, and think well of every task from cleaning the restrooms to praying and preaching the Word. One day, you too will see the eyes of the dead opening to life again.

97

Priority #1: Worship and Thanksgiving

So she went in, fell at his feet, and bowed to the ground; then she picked up her son and went out.

II Kings 4:37 NKJV

As each of their children approached high school graduation my parents took the family on a celebratory road trip around a portion of the United States. For my older sister's trip we went west to places like Great Sand Dunes National Park, Arches National Park, and Carlsbad Caverns to name but a few locales that gave me a love for the vast open spaces the West has to offer. For my trip my father planned an Appalachian Trail themed trip where we would go up and down the East Coast rafting, hiking, and canoeing, all things I loved to do. One of the highlights of the plan was a hike up Mt. Washington in New Hampshire. However, upon arriving at the base of the mountain in somewhat overcast weather and with young siblings, I became very ungrateful at his plan and rather than thank my father for all the work and logistics to give us this opportunity I complained.

Thankfully, my father did not react to my unthankfulness as I deserved by calling it a day and abandoning the plan but rather he pushed us forward, and all of us hiked to the top of Mt. Washington. Most of the family took a shuttle down the mountain from the summit, but my father and I hiked back down the mountain via a different trail. It ended up being one of my favorite memories and a fantastic time with my family and especially my father, and it gave me a love for the mountains that only continues to grow today. But with these things, I will never forget my sinful attitude and complaining, a mark of sinful men in these last days (2 Timothy 3:2).

We see this attitude around us regularly. Gifts given without even a word of thanks in return. We see complaining in all circumstances whether we have little or we have much. We grumble over the slightest unpleasantness in life and the wicked will even grumble and complain in the hour of their death. When ten lepers were healed only one turned around to thank the Lord Jesus. When the man with the withered hand was healed, many witnesses responding by planning how to destroy Jesus. Ungrateful, unthankful, these are the marks of the world and too often, like in my case, they abide even with God's people. But such is not to be the case: "And let the peace of God rule in your hearts to the which also ye are called in one body; and be ye thankful" (Col. 3:15).

Consider the actions of the Shunammite woman whose son had died. Her response to the Lord raising her son may be the greatest lesson she left with us. She did not run into the room and pick up her son with the warmest embrace she had ever given. She did not shout in disbelief and joy at him who was dead now alive again in her home. Before all this, she humbled herself before the Lord and His prophet and gave thanks to the Lord: "So she went in, fell at his feet, and bowed to the ground..." She was thankful! The Lord who had given her a great blessing restored that blessing to her again, and she did not relish first in the blessing but thanked the Lord who blessed her. She did not worship or praise her son but worshipped and praised the God who gave her son life from the dead!

There is a tremendous lesson here about worship. Why do we make a joyful shout to the Lord, go before the Lord's presence with singing, remember that the Lord, He is God, remember that He made us and not we ourselves, enter into His gates with thanksgiving, go into His courts with praise, be thankful to Him and bless His name (Ps. 100:1-4)? Why do we do these things and delight to do them? "For the Lord is good; His mercy is everlasting, and His truth endures to all generations" (Ps. 100:5).

The Lord has given us life, so the first priority in our lives on day one of the week is to worship the Lord. The Lord has given us new life in Christ, raising our dead souls to life eternal so we give thanks to Him, we bless His name as the highest priority in our life. Before hugging her son, the Shunammite gave thanks to the Lord; how much more ought we give thanks to the Lord in worship as the highest priority of our lives, for He has given us eternal life!

There is then a warning here. If we rush in to receive the blessings of the Lord and forget to worship Him as He rightly deserves and calls us to, are we thankful to the Lord? Do we know and understand the great gift that has been given to us? If we neglect the worship of God and choose other things above or before His worship, what does that say about our hearts toward the Lord and giver of life? The dead son of this woman had been raised to life and was sitting up in bed in front of her and she did not first run to him but rather gave thanks to God. Let us joyfully give first priority to the worship and praise of God in our lives who has done all things well. Let us enter into His gates with thanksgiving and into His courts with praise! Give thanks to Him; bless His name!

98

"Women Received Their Dead Raised To Life Again"

So she went in, fell at his feet, and bowed to the ground; then she picked up her son and went out.

II Kings 4:37 NKJV

What is faith? The world asks Christians this regularly. Can you answer? How is the Christian faith different from the Muslim faith or the Buddhist faith? Is it different? In the New Testament the Lord speaks of faith in a way that is unique to Christianity. In Hebrews 11, the Lord teaches us what faith is by giving a history of faith from the Old Testament saints. We sometimes call this chapter the "Hall of Faith" because it highlights those who lived their lives in faith to the Lord. Is there a hall of justification or a hall of sanctification? They are taught in different ways but faith is taught in this unique way by showing us those who lived by faith in Jesus Christ.

Hebrews 11 begins by telling us very simply what faith is: "Now faith is the substance of things hoped for, the evidence of things not seen... By faith we understand that the worlds were framed by the Word of God, so that the things which are seen were not made of things which are visible... Without faith it is impossible to please Him, for he who comes to God must believe that He is, and that He is a rewarder of those who diligently seek Him." Then the chapter launches into names and acts of men and women of faith: Abel, Enoch, Noah, Abraham, Sarah, Moses, Rahab, so many names time would fail us to recount them all but suffice it to say by faith, all those mentioned, "subdued kingdoms, worked righteousness, obtained promises, stopped the mouths of lions, quenched the violence of fire, escaped the edge of the sword, out of weakness were made strong, became valiant in battle, turned to fight the armies of the aliens. **Women received their dead raised to life again"** (vs. 35 emphasis added).

Through faith, women received their dead raised to life again. This only happened twice in the Old Testament both in the days of Elijah and Elisha with the widow of Zarephath and the Shunammite woman. Through faith in the Lord Jesus Christ, these women received their dead sons raised to life again.

This is no small account recorded in an obscure chapter of II Kings! The raising of the Shunammite woman's son from the dead teaches us about saving faith in the Lord Jesus Christ. Those who have this faith spoken of in Hebrews 11, sometimes called saving faith to differentiate from worldly faiths, have this trait: They receive and rest upon Christ alone for salvation as He is freely offered to us in the gospel. Through this same faith that we have now, by the grace and mighty power of the same Lord that we worship now, the Shunammite woman's son was raised from the dead and she is set up for us as an example of faith for all generations to emulate.

Do you have faith in Jesus Christ today? Are you resting in Him alone for salvation as He is freely offered in the gospel? There are many false Christs being presented in the world today. None of them have power to raise the dead. The Christ of Scripture alone has all power in Heaven and on Earth. Believe in Him alone today. Trust in Him alone today. Rest in Him alone today. Everyone else and everything else will let you down. But those who have faith in the Lord Jesus Christ alone will never be let down. For through faith women received their dead raised to life again!

99

Women Will Receive Their Dead Again!

So she went in, fell at his feet, and bowed to the ground; then she picked up her son and went out.

II Kings 4:37 NKJV

After the children of Israel crossed over the Jordan River in Joshua 4 and were on the plains of Jericho, the Lord told them to take twelve stones and set them up in Gilgal as a memorial to what the Lord had done by dividing the Jordan River. Why did the Lord require this? So that in years to come children would ask their fathers, "What are these stones?" The fathers would then tell their children that the Lord held back the Jordan so that the Israelites crossed over on dry ground just as they had the Red Sea. So all the peoples of the earth (and all the children of the Israelites) would know that the hand of the Lord is mighty and might fear the Lord God forever![1]

Why does the Lord give us the account of the Shunammite woman's son being raised from the dead and highlight her faith in Hebrews 11? As the stones were a memorial for Israel to trust the Mighty Lord so the Shunammite's son was a memorial to teach us that women will once again receive their dead to life. There were only a handful of times the Lord parted a river; there were only a handful of times that the Lord raised women's sons from the dead, but they are given as testimonies to us that we might not

---

[1] See Joshua 4 and also see similar passages concerning the testimonies and statutes of the Lord in Deuteronomy 6:20-25 and concerning the Passover in Exodus 12. The Lord is eager for the children and the children's children to the thousandth generation to know of His mighty works and deeds of old that they might fear Him and serve Him and rest in Him all of their days.

despair at the loss of loved ones but might know with certainty that the Lord will deliver the dead to life again.

The Lord loves His people very much. He does not want us to be ignorant concerning those who have died (fallen asleep) in the Lord lest we sorrow as those who have no hope. So in His infinite kindness and mercy He tells us that if we believe that Jesus died and rose again, even so will Jesus raise those who have died in the Lord. He is all powerful to raise the dead. The word of His power will raise the dead from their graves at the last day and we will be with the Lord forever. God has given us these words to comfort us and that we might comfort one another (I Thes. 4:13-18).

I suspect these words would have less impact on us if they came without the many historical examples of the Lord raising the dead. Putting together the promise of power with the actual demonstration of that power in the lives of His people we can have much comfort in the Lord our God. Just like the widow of Zarephath, the Shunammite woman, Jairus, the widow of Nain, Martha and Mary the sisters of Lazarus, so too we will one day receive our dead raised to life again. We will hold them, rejoice with them, but most of all worship the Lord with them. For when we behold those who were dead yet living again, we will behold something far greater: We will behold the Lord Jesus Christ who rose from the dead on the third day and never died again but ascended into Heaven and sat there until He descended from Heaven with a shout. As we behold the face of Him who reigns for ever and ever with all our tears wiped away, the ability to sin removed, and glorified bodies and souls, it will not be our loved ones that we first run to, but our Savior Jesus Christ before whom we bow and worship with thanksgiving!

Men and women, boys and girls, in the world we will surely have tribulation and trial, but be of good cheer, Christ has overcome the world! As women of old received their dead raised to life again, so you too will behold those have died in Christ raised to eternal life forevermore! Praise be to the Lord!

100

The Resurrection

So she went in, fell at his feet, and bowed to the ground; then she picked up her son and went out.

II Kings 4:37 NKJV

Every building that is expected to stand for a long time and resist the forces of wind and weather, the weight of snow and ice, must have an exceptionally strong foundation. No matter the visible grandeur of the construction, if the foundation is not strong, the building will not last. Take One World Trade Center in NYC for example. It stands more than 1,300 feet above street level even before taking into account its 400 foot spire. But you cannot see its foundation that descends 110 feet into the ground. As a strong tower must have a strong foundation, so the Christian faith must have a strong foundation if it is to stand the tests of time, the opposition of false religions, the doubters and deniers, and the devil who would oppose it.

Praise be to God, the Christian faith has a strong foundation, and its cornerstone is no mere rock or steel-reinforced concrete that can be broken but the eternal living and true God Man Jesus Christ. The core message of this faith is what Paul preached first, "That Christ died for our sins according to the Scriptures, and that He was buried, and that He rose again the third day according to the Scriptures..." (I Cor. 15:3-4).

The life, death, and resurrection of Jesus Christ is at the heart of Christianity, and without these there is no hope in this life and we are of all men most miserable for we have believed in vain. But the Lord is zealous throughout Scripture for His people to believe with certainty that Jesus did rise from the dead. Because He rose from the dead He has become the first fruits of them that sleep. Just as Christ rose from the dead, so He shall raise us up from the dead at the last day. The resurrection of Jesus Christ is at the heart and foundation of Christianity!

We have spent nearly 20 devotionals on the account of the Shunammite woman and her son, culminating in the Lord raising her son. What a great comfort and picture of what the Lord will do at the last day! However, the comfort of the Shunammite's raised son will fall short because eventually he died again. He is not with us now but fell asleep again many years later. The same can be said of all others whom the Lord raised from the dead in the Old and New Testaments. But the same is not the case for Jesus Christ. He who laid down His life and took it up again did not rise to mortality but to immortality. He rose to glory. He rose to power. He rose to intercede for us in Heaven from where He shall come again at the last day.

The resurrection of the Shunammite's son is not the center of the Christian faith. It is the resurrection of Jesus Christ that we find at the center. It is the center of all the apostles' teaching and the center of our lives. So central is it that on the day of Christ's resurrection, the first day of the week, the Lord's Day, we come into God's house to worship Him each and every week.

It is difficult, perhaps impossible, to overstate the importance of the resurrection of Christ. In the many sermons found in Acts, every single one makes its focus either explicitly or implicitly on the bodily resurrection of Jesus Christ. This is the heart of the Christian faith and the gospel message, that Jesus Christ lived, died, and rose again from the dead.

Is the resurrection of Jesus Christ the foundation of your life? Do you live your life believing that because Christ rose He will also raise the dead at the last day along with you and your loved ones if you die before He returns? Without the resurrection, the cross is worthless, for Christ would still be paying for sin. Without the resurrection, the virgin birth is meaningless because the sacrifice of the perfect Jesus did not yet make payment for our totally depraved bodies and souls. Without the resurrection, the Word of God is of little value because the promises have limited weight and glory behind them. Without the resurrection, there is no Christian religion or salvation.

"But now Christ is risen from the dead...." With the resurrection of Christ, all the work Christ came to do was completed. Salvation has been gained to the uttermost. Death is swallowed up in victory through the Lord Jesus Christ so that we can say with Paul, "O death where is your string? O Hades, where is your victory?" (I Cor. 15). With the resurrection of Christ, all power has been given to Christ in Heaven and on Earth so we can go forward, confessing Him before men, and serving Him without fear of the world, for He has overcome the world. Because Jesus is the Resurrection and the Life, though we may die, we shall live. And whoever lives and believes in Christ shall never die. Do you believe this (John 11:25)?

The Lord, He is God!

Made in the USA
Middletown, DE
04 November 2020

23318410R00157